must-see
BARCELONA

Published by Thomas Cook Publishing
A division of Thomas Cook Holdings Ltd
PO Box 227, Thorpe Wood
Peterborough PE3 6PU
United Kingdom

Telephone: 01733 503571
E-mail: books@thomascook.com

Text: © 2000 Thomas Cook Publishing
Maps: © 2000 Thomas Cook Publishing
Transport map: © TCS Ltd

ISBN 1 841570 67 2

Distributed in the United States of America by the Globe Pequot Press,
PO Box 480, Guilford, Connecticut 06437, USA.

Distributed in Canada by Whitecap Books, 351 Lynn Avenue,
North Vancouver, British Columbia, Canada V7J 2C4.

Distributed in Australia and New Zealand by Peribo Pty Limited,
58 Beaumont Road, Mt Kuring-Gai, NSW, 2080, Australia.

Publisher: Stephen York
Commissioning Editor: Deborah Parker
Map Editor: Bernard Horton

Series Editor: Christopher Catling

Written and researched by: Tony Kelly

Note: Throughout this book, Catalan is used for names and addresses and
most other words, but Spanish is given where that is more useful, such as in
the names of Spanish as opposed to Catalan dishes.

Cover photograph: Neil Setchfield

must-see BARCELONA

TONY KELLY

Getting to know Barcelona

Discovering Barcelona

If you had to pick one word to sum up the Catalan capital, the word would be 'style'. You see it in the art of Joan Miró, the genius of the Modernista architects, and the city's enduring obsession with design. You see it on La Rambla during the evening when people promenade in their smartest casuals, or sip cortados and talk politics at café tables out on the street. You see it in the flower stalls, in the window displays of pastry shops and in an appreciation bordering on reverence for the simple pleasures of life, from a plate of fresh seafood to a crusty loaf rubbed with tomato. You see it, too, at the Camp Nou, the cathedral of Catalan football, when a team founded by foreigners and still full of overseas stars goes out to represent Catalonia against the old enemy, Real Madrid.

For in all the excitement over Barcelona's art, architecture and street life, it is easy to overlook the most important fact about the city: it is the capital of Catalonia. The Catalans pride themselves on being different from other Spaniards, more businesslike, less flamboyant. This is not the region of flamenco and heel-clicking dances; the Catalan national dance is the sedate *sardana*, performed by a group of dancers holding hands in a ring. Nor is there any sympathy for the Spanish concept of *mañana*, the idea that everything can be put off until another day: the people of Barcelona will party all night, but they will be back at work in the morning. The cliché about the Catalans is that they work hard and play hard, their capacity for *rauxa* ('emotion') balanced by a basic *seny* ('common sense').

For much of its recent history, Catalonia has been suppressed, but in the new, democratic Spain it is holding its head up high. Since 1980, though everyone in Catalonia understands Spanish, the use of the regional language, Catalan, has become increasingly 'normalised'. The Catalan flag now flies from government buildings, and symbols of Catalan culture are everywhere. Even immigrants from other parts of Spain, who make up a high proportion of the population, tend to become adopted Catalans, learning the language, supporting Barça and dancing the *sardana* on Sundays.

Barcelona is more than just Spain's second city; throughout its history it has looked outwards to Europe as much as to the Iberian peninsula. In the Middle Ages it became a great port; now it is a dynamic business centre, as close to Paris and Milan as it is to Madrid. The city with an endless capacity for reinventing itself has now found a new role, as

the self-proclaimed 'capital of the Mediterranean', and there's a buzz about the place as it enters the new millennium. Modernist and Gothic, creative and chic, Barcelona is bursting with energy and fizzing with life like a bottle of Catalan Cava just waiting to explode.

BCN

In line with the fashion for rebranding and Barcelona's obsession with its own image, the city is increasingly referred to these days as BCN – a bizarre moniker derived from the international airline code for Barcelona.

Life in Barcelona

Like all Mediterranean people, the people of Barcelona know how to enjoy life – but they also know how to get things done. Perhaps that is why Barcelona was the engine of Spain's industrial revolution, and why Catalonia is the country's wealthiest region. Despite this success, they have the good sense to realise that there is no point in earning money if you cannot spare time for the really important things in life.

Morning

Some guidebooks will tell you that nothing happens in Spain before 1000. That is simply not true. Tourists may not be able to cope with a night at the disco and an early start, but most locals can. Even in summer, when some people adjust their timetable so that they work all morning and early afternoon, sleep all evening and dance all night, they come home from the nightclub and go straight to work. By 0800 the rush-hour is in full swing, the Metro trains are full and the markets are starting to get busy. Breakfast is a coffee and pastry at any time of the morning, or, for workers at the Boqueria market, an omelette and a nip of brandy at the bar. By 1000 the shops are open and bleary-eyed tourists are stumbling out of bed.

Afternoon

Lunch is a late and leisurely affair, beginning at around 1400. Shops and businesses close their doors and everyone goes home or decamps to the nearest restaurant. The tradition of the **siesta** was never as strong in Catalonia as in the warmer regions of southern Spain, and with Barcelona increasingly following European business hours it is in danger of dying out altogether, but although few people take a nap, most will still

> " *Barcelona, the treasure house of courtesy, the refuge of strangers, unique in its position and its beauty.* "
>
> **Miguel de Cervantes,**
> ***Don Quixote*, 1605**

have an hour or two off work. At weekends and in summer, this is the time for a long lunch by the sea or a picnic in the park followed by a rest in the shade.

Evening

As the shops reopen their doors, Barcelona spills out on to the street for the **early-evening *paseo***, that fine Spanish ritual of a casual stroll which provides an opportunity for gossip and flirtation once the heat of the day relents. By 1900 the bars are filling up, as people meet for a *copa* ('drink') and a snack. By 2100, most people are thinking about dinner, and others are on their way to the theatre. If FC Barcelona are playing, the streets will be quiet, the bars full of people watching the game on television, and you know if Barça has won from the sudden explosion of car horns at around 2300. By that time the *paseo* has ended, but there are still crowds on **La Rambla**, heading down towards the **discos of Port Vell**. When they go home, in the small hours of the morning, La Rambla will be deserted apart from a handful of newsstands and cleaners hosing down pavements in preparation for another day.

Yesterday and tomorrow

Although there is evidence of earlier civilisations on Montjuïc, Barcelona was probably founded by the Romans as the city of Barcino *in the 1st century* BC. *Captured by Visigoths, Moors and the Frankish emperor Charlemagne, it was brought under Catalan control in* AD *878, when* Wilfred the Hairy *became the first Count of Barcelona, ruling over an area similar in size to modern-day Catalonia and establishing a dynasty that lasted for 500 years. According to tradition, as Wilfred lay wounded in battle his lieutenant,* Charles the Bald, *dipped his fingers in the Count's blood and wiped them across his shield, creating the red and gold stripes of the Catalan flag.*

In 1137, Count Ramon Berenguer IV of Barcelona married the infant Petronilla of Aragón, uniting the two houses and ushering in Barcelona's Golden Age. The new kingdom became a major Mediterranean power, with conquests including Sicily, Naples and the Balearics. Catalan became the official language and the Generalitat (Catalan government) was set up.

But the marriage of Fernando of Aragón to Isabella of Castile in 1469 brought the kingdom of Aragón to an end, and the defeat of the Moors in Granada then led to the unification of Spain. In 1715, as punishment for supporting the Austrian claims during the War of the Spanish Succession, the Bourbon king Felipe V abolished

Catalan institutions and pronounced their language illegal. The fall of Barcelona on 11 September the previous year is still commemorated as Catalan National Day.

During the **industrial revolution** of the 19th century, Barcelona experienced rapid growth. The city walls were torn down, the **Rambla** was created and the **Eixample** was built to accommodate the rising population. At the same time, a revival of Catalan art and culture led to the rise of the *Modernista* movement.

The 20th century was a period of turmoil for Barcelona. In 1931, Catalonia declared its **independence** under the second Spanish Republic and was granted limited autonomy within Spain. During the Civil War (1936–9), Barcelona became the **Republican capital**; foreign volunteers, including the English writer George Orwell, flocked to the city to join the militias. When Franco's nationalists won, it was inevitable that he would take his revenge: the Catalan language was again banned and all expressions of solidarity suppressed during three decades of dictatorship. Unsurprisingly, Franco's death in 1975 was celebrated on the streets of Barcelona, and democracy and regional autonomy were restored. **Josep Tarradellas** made an emotional return after 40 years of exile to become president of the Generalitat. After elections in 1980, he was replaced by **Jordi Pujol**, who has held the job ever since and has also carved out a role for himself as a power-broker in national politics.

The **Olympic Games** of 1992 gave Barcelona the opportunity to show itself off to the world as the capital of a young, dynamic region, unleashing a building boom and a complete transformation of the waterfront, and the city is currently preparing for the Universal Forum of Cultures, to be held in 2004 on a derelict industrial site near the mouth of the Besòs river. The area is being completely rebuilt, and rechristened Diagonal-Mar.

" *I would rather be Count of Barcelona than King of the Romans.* "
Charles V, Holy Roman Emperor and King of Spain, 1519

People and places

The *Modernistas*

If one person has done more than any other to attract visitors to Barcelona, it is **Antoni Gaudí** (1852–1926),

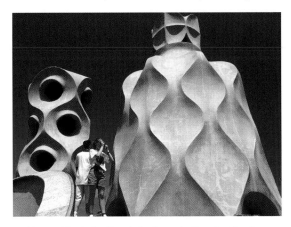

architect of Park Güell and the Sagrada Família. Gaudí was a key figure in the *Modernista* movement, a Catalan version of art nouveau which has been described as 'fairy-tale Gothic' after the way in which it took classic forms from Catalonia's Golden Age and reinvented them using mosaics, wrought iron and stained glass. Modernism (an imperfect translation, but one which for the sake of simplicity shall be used from now on) was closely linked with Catalan nationalism, whose symbols, such as the rose and the cross of St George, crop up repeatedly in Modernist art. In many ways, Gaudí was too individual to be considered a Modernist, and the more authentic figures are **Lluís Domènech i Montaner** (1850–1923), architect of the Palau de la Música Catalana, and **Josep Puig i Cadafalch** (1867–1957), designer of Picasso's favourite bar, Els Quatre Gats.

Art and design

Pablo Picasso, **Salvador Dalí** and **Joan Miró** are often held up as the 'holy trinity' of 20th-century Catalan artists, though only Miró spent much time in Barcelona. Picasso (1881–1973) was born in Málaga and moved to Barcelona at the age of 13, staying for nine years, though the city remained an important influence on his work. Dalí (1904–89) lived in northern Catalonia, while Miró (1893–1983) was born in

Barcelona and remained close to the city, contributing several public artworks and establishing the museum which bears his name. Barcelona's best-known living artist is **Antoni Tàpies** (b 1923), known for his abstract paintings and collages. The sculptor **Josep Maria Subirachs** (b 1927) also lives in the city and is responsible for the controversial figures on the Passion façade of the Sagrada Família. In a city obsessed with image, designers are also celebrities, none more so than **Xavier Mariscal** (b 1950), creator of the design bars of the 1980s and Cobi the Olympic mascot.

Literature and music

Manuel Vázquez Montalbán (b 1939) is Catalonia's best-known novelist, author of the Pepe Carvalho series of detective novels set in Barcelona. He lives in the city, supports FC Barcelona and writes a regular column for *El País*. The operatic soprano **Montserrat Caballé** (b 1933) is native to the city, taking her name from the holy mountain of Montserrat. Once a regular performer at the Liceu, she was active in the campaign to restore the opera house following the disastrous fire in 1994.

Politics and power

Jordi Pujol (b 1930) was imprisoned in 1960 for organising the singing of a Catalan anthem during a visit to the city by Franco, but in 1974 he launched the centre-right Catalan nationalist party CiU (Convergència i Unió), and by 1980 he was president of the Generalitat, a position he has held ever since. His period of office coincides with that of **Josep Lluís Nuñez** (b 1931), president of FC Barcelona and arguably the second most powerful man in Catalonia. Born in Bilbao, he made his fortune in construction in Barcelona during the Franco years and was elected president by the club's membership in 1978, although he has now announced he will stand down by the end of 2000.

> " *A people is a fact of mentality, of language, of feelings. Finally it is a fact of will. The first characteristic of a people has to be the will to exist. It is this will, more than anything else, that assures the survival and blossoming of a people.* "

Jordi Pujol, president of Catalonia

Getting around

Barcelona is a compact city for getting about, and the lower end of town around **La Rambla** and the **Barri Gòtic** is best explored on foot. Beyond Plaça de Catalunya, the grid plan of the **Eixample** takes over, interrupted only by the broad sweep of Avinguda Diagonal. The rigid layout of the Eixample makes maps easy to follow, but distances are greater and the repetitive nature of the street plan can soon tire you out. If you want to visit some of the more outlying sights, you will need to use public transport.

The majority of local transport, including underground trains (**Metro**) and **buses**, is operated by the city transport authority TMB. There is also a suburban train network, Ferrocarrils Generalitat de Catalunya (**FGC**), run by the Catalan government. The two systems are integrated and you can switch easily from one to the other, but for single journeys you must buy a separate ticket. If you plan on doing much travelling by public transport, your best bet is to buy a **T-1** ticket, valid for ten journeys on Metro, buses or FGC. You must validate your card each time you travel by inserting it into the turnstile at Metro stations or the machine behind the driver's carriage on buses. There is also a one-day pass (**T-DIA**) valid on all three networks, but, infuriatingly, the three- and five-day passes are valid on Metro and buses only. Children under four travel free of charge; after that age the full adult fare must be paid. Another option is the Barcelona Card, available from tourist offices, which gives free public transport and discounts at museums, attractions and shops for 24, 48 or 72 hours.

Rollerblading

If you want to look like a local, hire a pair of blades and get down to the waterfront promenade at weekends. Most of the hire shops are situated close to the Olympic port.

Metro and FGC

For most journeys within Barcelona, the Metro is the fastest and most reliable way of getting about. Throughout this book, where a sight is located close to a Metro station, the name of the station has been given; bus routes are only listed if the Metro is not convenient. There are five different lines, numbered and colour-coded, and you can pick up a map of the system at any Metro station. Trains are indicated by the name of the station at the end of the line in the direction in which they are travelling; for example, if you want to go from Sants-Estació to Sagrada Família on line 5, you need to follow the signs for Horta. FGC lines are marked on the same map as the Metro, and provided you have the right ticket the difference need not concern you.

Surprisingly for Barcelona, the big drawback of the Metro system is that it shuts down early, making it impractical for a night out at the theatre or even a late dinner. Standard hours are Monday to Thursday 0500–2300, Friday and Saturday 0500–0200 and Sunday 0600–0000, with extensions for festivals and evening football matches. During these times the trains run approximately every five minutes, so you never have to wait long.

Buses

The advantage of buses is that they enable you to see the sights en route; they also cover a wider area than the Metro, reaching out into the suburbs to places like Park Güell and Tibidabo. The disadvantage is that they tend to be slower, though special bus lanes mean they do not often get held up in traffic. Buses are certainly a useful option for one-off journeys between the centre and the outlying areas, but not so good if your journey is not covered by a single route. With the Metro, you can go into any Metro station and travel to any other on a single ticket, even if it involves a change of trains; with buses this is far more complicated and usually involves paying twice. There is a network of night buses centred on **Plaça de Catalunya**, useful if you are caught out after the Metro has closed. T-1 and T-DIA tickets are not valid on night buses.

Barcelona

Bus Turístic

These open-top tour buses leave Plaça de Catalunya at regular intervals, starting at 0900 and continuing to 1800 or later. The **northern (red) route** follows a circuit around the Eixample and out to Tibidabo and Pedralbes; the **southern (blue) route** takes in Montjuïc and the waterfront. The two routes, each of which takes around 90 minutes in total, intersect at three different places, so you can switch easily from one to the other. The ticket, available from tourist offices or on the bus, is valid for one or two days and you can hop on and off as often as you like, combining a scenic tour of the city with visits to some of the outlying sights. If you plan to do this, the two-day ticket is better value. The ticket comes with a discount booklet offering substantial reductions on various museums and attractions, which do not have to be used up on the same day. It is just about possible to recoup the full cost of your ticket if you take advantage of all these savings.

Taxis

Black-and-yellow taxi cabs are everywhere in Barcelona; you can hail one on the street when you see a green light on the roof and a sign in the windscreen saying *LLIURE* or *LIBRE*. There are also taxi ranks at major railway stations and squares, including Plaça de Catalunya. Taxis are allowed to use bus lanes, so they get around quickly. Prices are reasonable and are

displayed in English inside the cab, with supplements for weekends, public holidays and late-night rides. A tip of 5–10 per cent is generally acceptable, but be warned: taxi drivers are not legally obliged to carry more than 2 000 pesetas in change.

Joyrides

Besides trains, buses and taxis, Barcelona has several enjoyable ways of getting about. Chief among these are the **Golondrinas boat trips** (*see page 98*) and **Tibidabo tram and funicular** (*see page 140*). There is also a funicular railway which travels up the steep hillside from the Paral.lel Metro station to Montjuïc, connecting with a cable-car to the summit. All of these joyrides operate daily in peak season, but in winter are usually only open at weekends. The most thrilling ride of all, a cable-car journey across the port from Barceloneta to Montjuïc on the *transbordador* (a relic of the 1929 International Exhibition), has been closed for repairs for several years, but there are still hopes that it may be revived. In summer there is a miniature road train from Plaça

17

d'Espanya to Montjuïc – an ascent that can also be made on foot using Barcelona's unique outdoor escalators.

Walking and cycling tours

A two-hour walking tour of the Barri Gòtic leaves on Saturday and Sunday mornings at 1000 from the tourist office on Plaça de Catalunya. Numbers are limited, so it is essential to book in advance. For a tour of Barcelona with a difference, join one of the guided cycling tours operated by **Un Cotxe Menys** (*Carrer Esparteria 3; tel: 93 268 2105*), a bicycle hire shop whose name means 'one car less'.

Don't miss

1 La Rambla

Can there be a street anywhere in the world that sums up an entire city better than La Rambla? From flower stalls and cafés to the endless parade of street life, a walk along La Rambla is the best possible introduction to Barcelona and its sense of style. **Pages 20-33**

2 Barri Gòtic

In a city obsessed with modernity, a stroll around the Gothic Quarter is a step back in time, as you stumble across hidden churches, ancient squares and medieval palaces with coats of arms above the door. **Pages 48-61**

3 Museu Picasso

The artist Pablo Picasso spent his early years in Barcelona and the Catalans like to claim him as one of their own. A visit to this museum gives an insight into his early life and the experiences that were to influence much of his later work. **Pages 70-1**

4 Parc de la Ciutadella

Barcelona's central park was designed for the 1888 World Fair, with architecture by **Gaudí** and **Domènech i Montaner**. Although it contains a zoo and a number of museums, most people come here to relax among the fountains, gardens and lakes. **Pages 90-1**

5 Fundació Joan Miró

You cannot escape Joan Miró in Barcelona – his colourful, childlike images are everywhere and seem to epitomise the city's sense of fun. This fascinating museum contains a selection of his paintings and sculptures in a bright, modern setting. **Pages 106-7**

6 Museu Nacional d'Art de Catalunya

The Catalan art museum houses the greatest collection of **Romanesque art** in Europe, most of it salvaged from remote Pyrenean churches on the medieval pilgrim route to Santiago de Compostela. **Pages 110-11**

7 Casa Milà

This apartment block by **Gaudí** is a good place to begin a tour of Barcelona's Modernist architecture. The building contains many typical Gaudi touches, and there is an exhibition on his life and work in the loft. **Pages 120-1**

8 Sagrada Família

The symbol of Barcelona is this extraordinary unfinished cathedral, to which **Gaudí** devoted half of his life. Long after his death, the work goes on, and the arguments rage over Gaudi's artistic legacy. **Pages 126-7**

9 Park Güell

Whatever you think of Gaudi, it is hard not to be enchanted by this playful park, with its fairy-tale pavilions, a dragon stairway and a twisting mosaic bench. **Pages 138-9**

10 Camp Nou

For anyone outside Spain, it is hard to understand the significance to Catalans of Barcelona football club. The Camp Nou is not just Europe's largest football stadium; it is a shrine to the Catalan nation and a worldwide symbol of the region's success. **Pages 144-5**

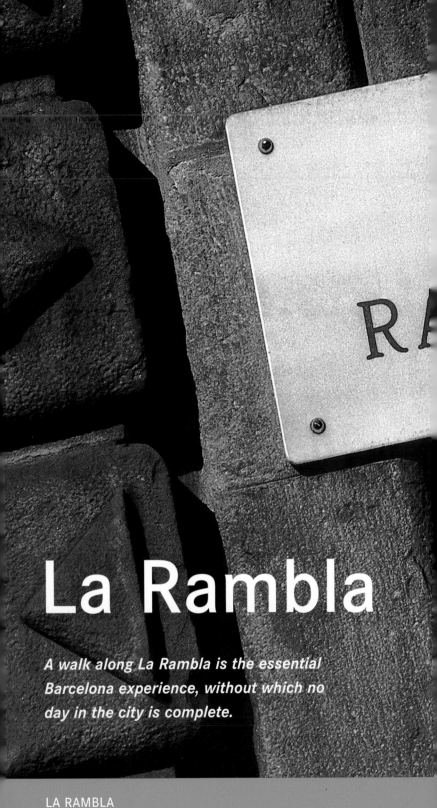

La Rambla

A walk along La Rambla is the essential Barcelona experience, without which no day in the city is complete.

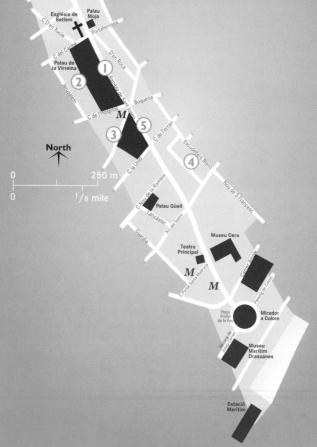

Getting there: *Plaça de Catalunya, at the top end of La Rambla, is Barcelona's main public transport hub and the departure point for the Bus Turístic. Catalunya Metro station is situated beneath the square. Other useful Metro stations are Liceu, midway along La Rambla, and Drassanes, at the seaward end.*

Ronda de Sant Pere

M ⑥

i

Av Portal de l'Àngel

C Universitat

Bergara

La Rambla

C dels Tallers

C Canuda

Elisabets

Església de Betlem

Palau Moja

C D'en Xuclà

Portaferrissa

C del Carme

D'en Roca

Palau de la Virreina

① ②

Jerusalem

Rambla de Sant Josep

Boqueria

C de l'Hospital

M

⑤

③

C de Ferran

North

C la Unió

Escudellers Blanc

④

Nou de S Francesc

0 ———— 250 m

0 ———— 1/8 mile

C Nou de la Rambla

C Nou de la Rambla

Palau Güell

Lancàster

Arc del Teatre

Guàrdia

Museu Cera

Teatro Principal

M

C Santa Madrona

M

Cerera Ampla

Passeig de Colom

Plaça Portal de la Pau

Mirador a Colom

Av Drassanes

Museu Marítim Drassanes

Estació Marítim

① La Rambla street life

The whole point of La Rambla is its endless parade of street life, from the buskers and the performance artists who can stand still for hours to the colourful flower and bird stalls and the transvestite prostitutes who give the street its rougher edge. **Pages 24-7**

② La Boqueria

Barcelona's central market is a riot of colours, tastes and smells, busy from morning till night. Come here to buy bread, cheese, olives and fruit for a picnic, or to admire the staggering array of fresh seafood and the variety of Catalan sausages. **Page 26**

③ Gran Teatre de Liceu

Barcelona's opera house is open once again and has returned to its place at the heart of the city's cultural life. Destroyed by fire in 1994, it has been sympathetically restored, with the addition of some controversial new ceiling paintings. **Page 28**

④ Plaça Reial

Despite a heavy police presence and a reputation for sleaze, this handsome arcaded square with its sunny café terraces remains one of the best spots in the city for people-watching. It also contains Antoni Gaudí's earliest known work in Barcelona. **Page 29**

⑤ Café de l'Opera

This gilded and wood-panelled coffee house is a Barcelona institution, founded in 1929 and still going strong. Come here during the day to sit outside on La Rambla, or late at night to take part in a post-opera artistic discussion. **Page 30**

⑥ Plaça de Catalunya

With sculptures, fountains and gardens, this popular meeting-point is the nearest thing in Barcelona to a central square. Situated at the top of La Rambla, it marks the divide between the historic city and the 19th-century Eixample ('extension') to the north. **Pages 32-3**

Tourist information

Barcelona's main tourist information centre is situated beneath Plaça de Catalunya (*open: 0900–2100 daily; closed 1 Jan and 25 Dec*). As well as general information, it offers walking tours, currency exchange, a hotel booking service, Internet access and a gift shop.

Tip

La Rambla is perfectly safe for strolling, but petty street crime is prevalent and it is important to stay alert. Keep an eye out for bag-snatchers, and never leave your wallet or camera out on a café table on the street. Although the street life is all part of the fun, it is best to avoid unlicensed vendors who try to sell you flowers, and the tricksters and con artists who set up card games on the pavement.

A stroll along La Rambla

The author Manuel Vázquez Montalbán has called it 'a metaphor of life'; for the poet Federico García Lorca it was 'the only street in the world which I wish would never end'. Sooner or later, and probably sooner, every visitor to Barcelona is going to end up walking La Rambla, a boulevard which seems to sum up the entire city. There is even a word for it: ramblejar, *meaning to stroll along La Rambla, as the locals do by day and by night, and especially on weekend afternoons.*

The name has its origins in a dried-up river bed – almost every Catalan town has one, but Barcelona's is the best known. In medieval times this was the city's western boundary, lined with monastic buildings and defensive walls. The walls were demolished in the 18th century and the first street lamps were put up, turning La Rambla into a **popular promenade**. The street that you see today was largely complete by 1860, when plane trees were imported from La Devesa park in Girona and cast iron was used to build the flower stalls and newspaper kiosks which provide so much of the street's colour and life.

Traffic is now allowed to pass along either side, but this is one street in Barcelona where the pedestrian reigns supreme, most of the action taking place on the wide central pavement. La Rambla is just over a kilometre (two-thirds of a mile) long; although it is split into five distinct sections, most people refer to the entire street as La Rambla.

" *The women, beautiful, graceful and coquettish, preoccupied by the fold of their mantillas and the play of their fans; the men by their cigars, as they strolled along, laughing, chatting, ogling the ladies, discussing the opera, and seeming not to care in the least what might be happening beyond the city walls.* "

George Sand on La Rambla, *Winter in Majorca*, 1855

You could start at the seaward end, standing beneath the **Mirador a Colom** ('Monument to Columbus') with your back to the port. Heading inland, **Rambla de Santa Mònica** takes its name from a former convent on this site, converted into an arts centre during the 1980s as part of a plan to clean up what had become a sordid stretch used for highly visible drug-dealing and prostitution. The area is still patrolled by prostitutes (many of them transvestites) and pickpockets after dark, but it is nowhere near as rough or as threatening as it was, and for the savvy and broad-minded visitor it is no more than a mildly entertaining spectacle. A craft market is set up here on the street at weekends.

Further up the street are the portrait painters, who can rustle up a good likeness or caricature in no time. You can even leave them a photograph of a loved one and return in a couple of hours to pick up the portrait. At weekends the artists are joined by an assortment of charlatans, including fortune-tellers and tarot-readers.

Passing the **Teatre Principal**, built in 1847 on the site of Barcelona's first theatre, you reach the **Rambla dels Caputxins**, the start of the long, straight section which runs all the way to Plaça de Catalunya. Look up to your left to admire the **mosaic façade** of the Ramblas Hotel. The hotels along here, such as the Oriente, were once *the* places to stay in Barcelona – writers such as **Ernest Hemingway** and **Federico García Lorca** have gazed down from their balconies. These days they appeal mainly to those who find romance in faded decadence and barely concealed sleaze.

La Rambla II

You are now approaching the most animated stretch of La Rambla, where buskers and magicians compete for attention with Barcelona's famous 'living statues'. These performance artists, spray-painted and made up to look like everyone from Roman soldiers to Count Dracula, can hold their silent poses for a remarkable length of time, springing to life only when a passer-by drops some coins into their box. To watch it all happening, take a seat on the promenade outside the Café de l'Opera (*see page 30*), across the street from the restored Liceu opera house (*see page 28*).

The action reaches a peak at Pla de l'Os, the halfway point of La Rambla, marked by a mosaic pavement designed by Joan Miró in 1976. Near here, look out for the Modernist shopfronts of Caixa de Sabadell (*No 82*), adorned with a Chinese dragon, and Antiga Casa Figueras (*No 83*), now Escriba, a celebrated pastry-shop across the street (*see page 31*).

A short way up on the left, La Boqueria is Barcelona's main market, also known as Mercat Sant Josep (*open: Mon–Sat 0800–2100*). For serious gourmets, this is a feast for the eyes. Some of Catalonia's freshest produce is sold here: hanging hams and sausages greet you at the entrance, along with colourful fruit and vegetable stalls; fresh fish and seafood are arranged in a circle at the centre, with stalls devoted to eggs, cheese, olives and wild mushrooms. There are also stand-up *tapas* bars where the workers drink beer and demolish tripe for breakfast.

The market stands near the start of Rambla de Sant Josep, usually known as Rambla de les Flors because of the picturesque flower stalls which line the promenade well into the evening. The florists are the best-known and best-loved image of La Rambla, recalled in a popular song of the 1940s

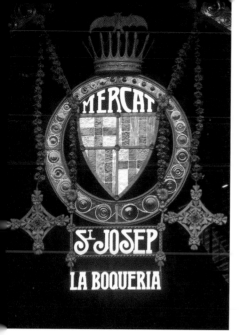

which paid tribute to the legendary beauty of its flower girls: 'How lovely is Barcelona, pearl of the Mediterranean, how lovely it is to stroll, and watch the women on the Rambla de les Flors'. Almost as well known are the newspaper vendors, some open 24 hours a day, selling newspapers from all over Europe on the day of publication, as well as a staggering variety of pornography. Be warned: they do not take kindly to people flicking through the merchandise without paying.

In your efforts to enjoy the street life, try not to ignore the buildings. On the left, the **Palau de la Virreina** is a splendid neo-classical palace, built for the Viceroy of Peru and now used as an exhibition centre. It is followed by the baroque façade of the **Betlem church** Across the street is another 18th-century palace, **Palau Moja** now the Catalan government bookshop (*see page 31*). As you reach Rambla dels Estudis, named after an old university, look up to your left at the **colonial-style façade** of the old Philippine tobacco company. Along this stretch, also known as **Rambla dels Ocells** ('birds'), flowers give way to songbirds and stalls selling pets from goldfish to tortoises and guinea pigs.

> " La Rambla is the paradise of possibilities, one of those places in which you need to pinch yourself and blink several times in order to believe that its assorted posers, magicians, actors and grotesques are genuinely before you. "
>
> **Jonathan Keates, *World*, 1992**

Finally, you reach **Rambla de Canaletes**, a wide, open space with metal chairs for hire. The small fountain here is where supporters of FC Barcelona gather before and after important matches. According to legend, whoever drinks from the Canaletes fountain is sure to return to Barcelona.

Gran Teatre de Liceu

Rambla 51–9. Tel: 93 485 9900; www.liceubarcelona.com. Metro: Liceu. Open: 0945–1100 daily (last admission 1015). £. Box office open Mon–Fri 1400–2030 and one hour before performances at weekends.

The reopening of the Liceu opera house on 7 October 1999, more than five years after it was gutted by fire, marked a proud and significant moment in the cultural life of Barcelona. One of the first to give a recital was the Catalan diva **Montserrat Caballé**; before that, the theatre had symbolically reopened with Puccini's *Turandot*, the opera that had been due to play on the night of the fateful fire.

> " *Barcelona … a place of commerce where the stranger is not wanted unless he has something to sell cheaply, or desires to buy. A city of furtive, mannerless men who eye your money-pocket or watch a woman's handbag like hungry animals, and slovenly, uncorseted, unbeautiful women whose eyes seldom smile.* "
>
> **Gordon West, *Jogging Round Majorca*, 1929**

This was not the first time that tragedy had struck the Liceu. Opened in 1847 and modelled on La Scala in Milan, this was the second largest opera house in Europe when the original building was destroyed by fire in 1861. Then in 1893, an anarchist named Santiago Salvador threw two bombs into the stalls during a performance of Rossini's *William Tell*, killing 20 people. He was executed a month later.

If you cannot get to a performance, it is still worth visiting in order to see **Spain's finest opera house** restored to its original splendour. The style of the old theatre is best preserved in the **Saló dels Miralls** ('Hall of Mirrors') above the entrance foyer, with its gold leaf, frescos and enigmatic inscriptions such as *La Comedia es el Espejo de la Vida* ('Comedy is the Mirror of Life'). The main auditorium has been authentically re-created, with gilded balconies and plush red velvet, as well as some extraordinary new ceiling paintings by the Catalan artist **Perejaume**, with computer-generated images of thousands of opera seats depicted in a mountain landscape.

Plaça Reial

Metro: Liceu.

Sitting outside one of the cafés on this **attractive porticoed square**, sipping a milky coffee and admiring the graceful fountain at its centre, it seems like the most perfect place in Barcelona – until someone sidles up to you and offers to sell you some hashish. Once a notorious drug-dealing spot, the square has been cleaned up considerably in recent years, but it retains a rough edge and an atmosphere of suppressed tension. Shady characters hang around its corners, the police are out in force, and although sheer weight of numbers means that you are generally quite safe here, it pays to remain on your guard.

The square, inspired by the large public spaces of France and Italy, was built in 1848 on the site of a Capuchin convent. The lamp-posts to either side of the fountain were designed by **Antoni Gaudí** in 1878, his first known work in Barcelona. Plaça Reial lies at the heart of La Mercè district, the seaward end of the Barri Gòtic as it drifts down towards the port. This was a fashionable 18th-century neighbourhood that fell into decline and is now, almost inevitably, on the way up again.

At night, this is one of the liveliest spots in Barcelona, with numerous discos, jazz clubs and bars. On Sunday mornings it is taken over by a large second-hand market specialising in stamps and coins.

Restaurants

Amaya
Rambla 20. Tel: 93 302 1037. £££.
Despite being situated at the lower,
seedy end of La Rambla, this Basque
restaurant is one of the best in the city,
popular with businessmen, politicians
and opera singers who come to enjoy
Basque classics such as grilled sea-
bream and fritters of hake throat.

Les Quinze Nits
Plaça Reial 6. Tel: 93 317 3075. £.
No bookings. The queues across the
square at weekends testify to the
popularity of this restaurant, which
offers solid Catalan cuisine at excellent
prices. Arrive early for one of the
outdoor tables on the square.

Taxidermista
Plaça Reial 8. Tel: 93 412 4536. ££.
Housed in an old taxidermist's studio
which Joan Miró and Salvador Dalí
used to visit, this trendy restaurant
offers contemporary versions of
Catalan cuisine, such as salt cod
with yucca crisps or duck breast
in truffle vinaigrette.

Cafés

Café de l'Opera
Rambla 74. This Modernist coffee
house, all dark wood and panelled
mirrors, has long been popular with
intellectuals who while away their
time over coffee and newspapers,
or hold *tertulias* ('literary debates'),
in the salon upstairs.

Café Moka
Rambla 128. In *Homage to Catalonia*,
George Orwell described a Civil War
shoot-out here from the relative safety
of a rooftop across the street. The café
is still there, with plenty of historical
atmosphere and a simple menu of
pizzas, paella, *tapas* and grills.

Pans & Company
Rambla 123. This sandwich chain, with
two outlets on La Rambla and others
across the city, has got fast food down
to a fine art, offering fresh baguettes
spread with tomato and fillings from
tortilla (potato omelette) to Spanish ham.

Shopping

Apart from La Boqueria market and the magnificent flower stalls, most of the shops on La Rambla are tourist traps selling tacky souvenirs and overpriced football shirts. There are, however, a few exceptions, which are well worth seeking out.

M Boué
Rambla 83. Established in 1870 and one of the oldest businesses on the street, this traditional cutler's shop sells knives, scissors and cleavers, handmade on the premises with handles fashioned from bull horns.

Casa Beethoven
Rambla 97. This small shop, founded in 1880, has the widest selection of sheet music in the city, from classical to rock music and Catalan *sardanas*. The wooden shelves give off a wonderfully old-fashioned aroma of sweet resin.

Escriba
Rambla 83. Once you have been drawn to this corner shop by its striking Modernist façade, take a look inside at the heavenly pastries, chocolates and cakes, sold in elegant gift boxes. You can also try them in the small café at the back of the shop.

La Botiga de la Virreina
Rambla 99. Situated inside the entrance to the Virreina palace, this museum shop features arty souvenirs and designer jewellery as well as a wide range of books on Barcelona's art and architecture.

Llibreria Generalitat de Catalunya
Rambla 118. The Catalan government bookshop, housed in an 18th-century palace, is a good source of English-language books about Catalonia, as well as maps, walking guides and Catalan dictionaries.

I Llobet
Rambla 129. It's worth going into this music shop just to see the leather-bound volumes of scores lining the shelves. It also sells musical instruments, such as Spanish guitars, maracas and the stringed instruments known as *lauds*, or lutes.

Market *músic*

Several stalls in La Boqueria market sell pa de figues *(* pan de higos *in Spanish), a tightly packed fig cake flavoured with almonds and cinnamon. Another variation on the same theme is the delightfully named* músic, *which can either be a solid wedge of dried fruit or a mixture of fruit and nuts in honey.*

Plaça de Catalunya

*This vast square at the top of La Rambla is the **symbolic centre of Barcelona**, where the narrow streets of the old town come up against the grid pattern of the 19th-century Eixample. When the medieval walls were finally demolished in 1859, Plaça de Catalunya was still a field outside the city; now it is the heartbeat of the city's life.*

Bus, train and Metro routes converge on the square, the tourist office is situated beneath it, and this is where people gather to gossip, flirt, talk football and hold political meetings.

LA RAMBLA

It was here in 1978 on La Diada, Catalonia's national day, that a massive demonstration of support for Catalan nationalism took place, shortly before the new statute of regional autonomy came into effect.

Although the first plans were developed in the mid-19th century, the square was not completed until 1927, when it was inaugurated by King Alfonso XIII. Most of the fountains and sculptures date from that time, including *Pastor tocant el flabiol* ('Shepherd playing the flute') by **Pau Gargallo** and a copy of **Josep Clarà**'s nude *Deessa* ('Goddess'), condemned as immoral when it first appeared. A more recent addition is *Catalunya a Francesc Macià*, a bust by Clarà of the former Catalan president and a modern 'interpretation' by the sculptor **Subirachs** which observers have likened to an upturned staircase.

> The principal landmark was the Hotel Colon, the headquarters of the PSUC … in a window, near the last O but one in the huge 'Hotel Colon' that sprawled across its face, they had a machine gun that could sweep the square with deadly effect.
>
> **George Orwell, *Homage to Catalonia*, 1938**

Of several banks that surround the square, the most notable is the **Banco Español de Credito** on the northern side, the headquarters of the Socialist party during the Civil War. George Orwell has described how its façade was covered with giant portraits of Lenin, Marx and Stalin – he would not recognise the square today. A branch of the English department store **Marks & Spencer** rubs shoulders with the **Hard Rock Café**, its incongruous slogan 'Save the Planet' emblazoned across its front. On one side of the square, the bleak concrete façade of **El Corte Inglés** hides Barcelona's best-known department store; across the square, the **El Triangle** shopping mall opened in 1999. The building of El Triangle entailed the demolition of **Café Zurich**, a much-loved meeting-point at the top of La Rambla, but the café is reborn at the entrance to the mall, its sunny terrace once again the best place to people-watch.

El Raval

Once a notorious slum district known as the Barrio Chino ('Chinatown'), this area has been transformed in recent years.

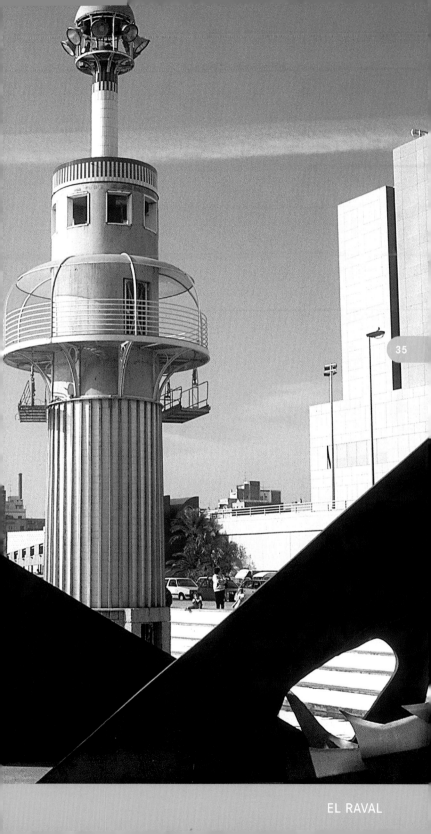

EL RAVAL

Getting there: the easiest entry to El Raval is from La Rambla, which gives access on foot to the district's main thoroughfares including Carrer del Carme, Carrer de l'Hospital, Carrer de Sant Pau and Carrer Nou de la Rambla. The most convenient Metro stations are Drassanes, Liceu and Paral.lel for the southern Raval, and Catalunya for the Museu d'Art Contemporani.

① Sant Pau del Camp

The oldest church in Barcelona dates from the 12th century, though there was a monastery on this site before then. The cloisters make a **peaceful retreat** from the chaos of the surrounding streets, and the shady gardens are a pleasant picnic spot.
Page 39

② Hospital de la Santa Creu

Once Barcelona's main hospital, this building now houses a library, an art gallery and various academic institutions. The **15th-century gardens**, surrounded by Gothic colonnades, are a haven of tranquillity, which seem a world away from the bustle of the streets outside. **Page 40**

③ Museu d'Art Contemporani de Barcelona

This sparkling white building is more than a museum, it is a symbol of the changes sweeping through El Raval. Its opening in 1995 marked the start of the revival that has turned a down-at-heel district into the most happening part of town. **Pages 40–1**

④ Palau Güell

The town house designed by **Antoni Gaudí** for his patron Eusebi Güell was one of his earliest works, and a visit here provides a glimpse into the early development of his style. The rooftop is pure Gaudi, with ceramic chimneys and a fairy-tale spire. **Pages 42–3**

⑤ Barrio Chino bars

The heyday of the Barrio Chino is long gone, but traces of the past linger on at a handful of decadent bars, survivors of an age when cabaret singers and good-time girls mingled with sailors, artists and foreigners eager for a glimpse of Barcelona low-life.
Page 45

⑥ Mercat de Sant Antoni

This wonderful **19th-century market hall** is many people's favourite in Barcelona, with much more of a local atmosphere than the more tourist-oriented La Boqueria. On Sundays it is the venue for a large second-hand book market.
Page 45

Tip

Despite recent changes, the southern half of El Raval is still a red-light district with the usual array of unsavoury characters. Take care in this area at night: stick to the main streets, avoid dark alleys and do not wear expensive jewellery or carry large sums of cash.

Barrio Chino

The reclaiming of El Raval from the ruins of the Barrio Chino is either a heartening tale of urban renewal or a depressing story of the destruction of a working-class neighbourhood. Built outside the city walls, this has always been a place on the margins, home to hospitals, factories, slaughterhouses and all those people and trades which did not fit in elsewhere.

> " *Cigarette girls, black marketeers, cripples, dope peddlers, vile, ill-lit bars, contraceptive shops, rooms let by the hour, six-peseta brothels, the entire Hispanic court of miracles imposed a brutal reality that burst the bubble around me with one blast.* "
>
> **Juan Goytisolo, *Forbidden Territory*, 1989**

Around 1925, when the district was one of the most crowded slums in Europe, a journalist named Àngel Marsà christened the place Barrio Chino ('Chinatown') because it reminded him of what he had heard of similar areas in the USA, with their neon signs, gangs and atmosphere of vice. Although there was probably not a single Chinese resident at the time, the name stuck, and it proved remarkably resilient. Foreigners were drawn by the seedy appeal of what novelist Camilo José Cela described as 'a heroic Numancia of cheap love and rough brandy'.

The *barrio* was a notorious red-light district; artists like **Picasso** frequented its brothels, and the French writer **Jean Genet** worked here as a rent boy, picking his customers' pockets and recounting his experiences in the autobiographical *Journal du Voleur* ('Thief's Journal'). People still come from overseas in search of the bohemian low-life, but these days they are mostly disappointed. Little remains of the Barrio Chino, though ironically there are Chinese residents these days. In fact, immigration has made this the most **multicultural district** of Barcelona, with halal butchers and Pakistani restaurants.

The demise of the Barrio Chino began during Franco's rule, when the Avinguda de les Drassanes swept through the southern half, destroying the most notorious slums. This process is continuing with an ambitious plan to create a Rambla-style promenade from the ring road to the port.

Entire blocks of housing are being ruthlessly demolished and their inhabitants relocated. Most people in Barcelona see this as a change for the better, but for others, the neighbourhood's character is being lost in the rush to accommodate tourists. Critics warn that you cannot make drugs and prostitution go away simply by tearing down blocks of flats.

For a last look at the Barrio Chino, start in La Rambla and walk down **Carrer Nou de la Rambla**. On your left is Gaudí's **Palau Güell** (*see pages 42–3*); across the street is **Viro's**, a typical old Raval shop where fancy dress costumes for children are sold alongside fantasy outfits for the local prostitutes. Further along the street, on the way to the Paral.lel music-hall district – a shadow of its former self, the chief attraction these days a hard-core porn show – shops sell lacy underwear, feathers and sequinned bras.

Turn right at the end of the street to reach **Sant Pau del Camp**, a peaceful Romanesque church shaded by palm trees. Note the **Visigothic columns** and the carvings above the portal, then wander inside to see the tombstone of Guifre II, founder of an earlier monastery on this site. Now take **Carrer de Sant Pau**, the main street of the Raval, where the recent changes are most visible despite traces of the past around the **Bar Marsella** (*see page 45*). Passing Hotel España, a **Modernist landmark** with a dining-room by Domènech i Montaner, turn left down a narrow alley to reach the church square of **Sant Agustí**. Beyond here, **Carrer de l'Hospital** marks the start of the northern Raval, always the more respectable district and now the epicentre for the revival of this quarter.

Hospital de la Santa Creu

Access from Carrer del Carme or Carrer de l'Hospital. Gardens open from 1000 to dusk. Admission free.

The peaceful gardens of this 15th-century hospital are one of the few remaining green spaces in El Raval, a treasured resource in an otherwise overcrowded neighbourhood. For more than 500 years this was the city's main hospital, until the opening of **Hospital de Sant Pau** (*see page 123*). It was here in 1926 that **Antoni Gaudí** died after being knocked down by a tram. The main hospital building is now the Biblioteca de Catalunya (Catalan Library) and the rest of the complex is given over to educational establishments, including the Institute of Catalan Studies, but if you try your luck you may be able to look around.

Glance into the vestibule of the **Casa de Convalescència**, richly decorated with ceramic tiles recording the life of St Paul, then seek out the **Colegi de Cirurgia** (College of Surgeons), with its oval operating theatre and revolving marble dissecting table. The hospital chapel is now **La Capella** (*Carrer de l'Hospital 56; open: Tue–Sat 1200–1400, 1600–2000, Sun 1100–1400; admission free*), a gallery used for exhibitions of contemporary art.

Museu d'Art Contemporani de Barcelona

Plaça dels Àngels 1. Tel: 93 412 0810; www.macba.es. Metro: Catalunya or Universitat. Open: Mon and Wed–Fri 1100–1930; Sat 1000–2000; Sun 1000–1500; closed Tue. ££ (half-price admission on Wed).

Richard Meier's contemporary art museum has done for El Raval what Frank Gehry's Guggenheim did for Barcelona's Basque rival Bilbao: it has provided a shining symbol of regeneration for a formerly run-down district trying hard to rebrand itself as a youthful centre of art and culture. It is impossible to exaggerate the importance of MACBA to this area since it opened in 1995. In a short time it has become one of the city's most visited attractions, bringing tourists not just to El Raval but to the inevitable cafés and art galleries which have followed in their wake. Just as important, it has become a defining image of the new, open Raval the authorities are attempting to create.

The building itself, all long ramps and luminous white walls with a huge glass façade, makes full use of natural light. The collection is focused on the second half of the 20th century, with an emphasis on Catalan and Spanish artists including **Antoni Tàpies**, **Perejaume**, **Miquel Barceló** and **Eduardo Chillida**. Most of the space is taken up with temporary exhibitions, including multimedia installations, but some of the permanent collection, beginning with works by **Alexander Calder** and **Paul Klee**, is usually on display on the ground floor.

The neighbouring **Centre de Cultura Contemporània de Barcelona** (*Carrer Montalegre 5; open: Tue, Thu, Fri 1100–1400, 1600–2000, Wed, Sat 1100–2000, Sun 1100–1900, closed Mon; ££*), housed in a former asylum known as Casa de la Caritat, is devoted to urban architecture and design. The building itself has been imaginatively converted, with parts of the original structure encased in glass around the central courtyard. Both museums have excellent shops selling modern design crafts, art books and souvenirs as well as original lithographs from contemporary Catalan artists.

Palau Güell

Carrer Nou de la Rambla 3–5. Tel: 93 317 3974. Metro: Liceu. Open: Mon–Fri 1015–1300, 1615–1830. £.

Antoni Gaudí was just 34 years old when he began work on the Güell palace, and a visit here provides an insight into the early development of his Modernist style. This was Gaudí's first major building in Barcelona, commissioned in 1886 by his patron **Count Eusebi Güell**, a wealthy industrialist and politician with a family home on La Rambla. The palace, linked to the house by an underground passage, would add to Güell's status and provide a suitable venue for the political meetings and concerts of chamber music such a man was expected to hold. Gaudí was the architect chosen to carry out the work, the start of a long and fruitful relationship which also produced **Park Güell** (*see pages 138–9*).

> " *As soon as I returned home, I smashed up the tiles in my bathroom to rearrange them trencadis fashion. It was an unmitigated disaster.* "
>
> **Paul Gogarty, *Barcelona and Catalonia*, 1993**

The Catalan coat of arms on the façade, fashioned out of wrought iron, provides a suitable introduction to the building, which in typical Gaudí style merges industrial materials (iron, brick, stone) and neo-Gothic elements with touches of Catalan patriotism. The main entrance takes the form of a **double vestibule**, designed to allow carriages to enter and leave through separate doors. Note the Scots pine flooring and the stone steps, carefully placed to assist visitors in mounting a horse or climbing into a coach. A ramp leads down to the old stables, whose brick columns and parabolic arches are reminiscent of Gaudí's later work at **Casa Milà** (*see pages 120–1*).

The house can only be visited on guided tours, which are justifiably popular, so arrive early in the day or be prepared to queue. Although there are few of the flights of fantasy associated with Gaudí's later work, his familiar themes are already starting to emerge. Amid the dark confines, mirrors and false windows are used to reflect light and give the impression of extra space. The central parlour, used for balls, concerts and religious events, is situated beneath a parabolic dome with small openings letting in the natural light in the manner of a Moorish bath-house.

The highlight of the visit is the climb to the roof terrace, with its decorated chimneys and fairy-tale spire with a weathervane in the shape of a dragon. The chimneys, which were comprehensively restored in 1992, are covered in *trencadis* (fragmented ceramic tiles) from local factories, as well as other materials including earthenware, marble and glass. Others retain their exposed brickwork, but in another Gaudiesque touch, their individual geometric shapes turn these plain functional objects into sculptures. From the terrace there are good views over the huddled buildings of El Raval and the wider city beyond.

The palace did not remain in the Güell family for long. During the Civil War, it was seized by the anarchists as their military headquarters; the stables became a prison, later taken over by Franco's police. For many years afterwards, the building housed Barcelona's theatre museum. In 1985, it became one of the first modern buildings anywhere in the world to gain Unesco World Heritage status.

EL RAVAL

Restaurants

Ca L'Isidre
*Carrer Les Flors 12. Tel: 93 441 1139.
£££.* This family-run restaurant in the
back streets of the Paral.lel music-hall
district is possibly Barcelona's finest,
patronised by King Juan Carlos and
Catalan president Jordi Pujol. The
style is classic Catalan with inventive
touches, and there is a superb all-
Catalan wine list.

Casa Leopoldo
*Carrer Sant Rafel 24. Tel: 93 441
3014. £££.* A well-known restaurant
specialising in seafood grills and top-
notch Catalan meat dishes, with no part
of the animal ignored: beef jawbones,
lamb's brains, tripe with *cap i pota*
(calf's head and foot).

L'Hortet
*Carrer Pintor Fortuny 32. Tel: 93 317
6189. Open for lunch and Fri–Sat
evenings. £.* This stylish vegetarian
restaurant has exposed brick walls
and an excellent four-course lunch
menu. It is very popular, so get here
early if you don't want to queue.

Silenus
*Carrer dels Àngels 8. Tel: 93 302 2680.
££.* One of several funky designer
restaurants to have opened near
MACBA, this features 'north–south'
Mediterranean cuisine with oriental
touches, such as turkey with mango,
chicken with dates, and salt cod with
aubergine caviar.

Cafés

Bar Ra
Plaça Gardunya. This cool café and
juice bar behind La Boqueria market
features an all-day menu of breakfasts,
snacks and eclectic Mexican-Thai-
Mediterranean cuisine, served at
outdoor tables on a sunny square.

Granja Viader
Carrer Xuclà 4. This legendary *granja*
or milk bar, founded in 1870, is just
the place for tea and cakes, or a mug
of hot chocolate with lashings of cream,
to keep you going during the long wait
for supper.

Rita Blue
Plaça Sant Agustí 3. This offbeat
designer bar, with Latin music,
Tex-Mex cuisine and modern art
on the walls, is a visible sign of
the gentrification that is sweeping
through El Raval.

Shopping

Many people prefer the **Mercat de Sant Antoni**, on the edge of El Raval, to the better-known Boqueria market on La Rambla. This fabulous market hall, dating from 1882, has more of a neighbourhood feel, with down-to-earth stalls selling fresh fish, slabs of pork and strings of tomatoes. Clothes stalls are set up around the edge several times a week, and on Sunday mornings there is a large second-hand book market featuring comics, coins and old film posters.

Tip

Amid all the changes to this district, look out for a pair of back-street shops, which have stood the test of time. El Indio (Carrer del Carme 24 *) is one of the city's gems, with a splendid Modernist shopfront and a cavernous interior, where carpets, rugs and rolls of cloth are packed into every space. Curtidos Pinós (* Carrer de l'Hospital 79 *), opposite Hospital de la Santa Creu, is an old-fashioned cobbler selling handmade boots and shoes, with drawers full of shoe polish and a fine collection of shoe-brushes in the window.*

Nightlife

Those in search of the Jean Genet experience can make a night-time tour of the last remaining vestiges of the Barrio Chino. You could start in the tiny **Bar Pastis** (*Carrer Santa Mònica 4*), opened in the 1940s by a Catalan artist who had lived in Marseille and wanted to recreate the atmosphere of the sailors' bars there. Bottles of Pernod line the shelves, Edith Piaf plays on the gramophone, the walls are stained with tobacco and transvestite prostitutes tap on the windows as they walk past. From here, head north to the **London Bar** (*Carrer Nou de la Rambla 34*), an old-time music pub with live bands most nights and occasional cabaret shows. Another survivor is **Marsella** (*Carrer de Sant Pau 65*), a decadent absinthe bar with a notice on one of the windows prohibiting singing. Although it is situated in one of the seediest parts of El Raval, this has become something of a tourist trap, popular with foreign students and daring young visitors keen to try out the potent green spirit. All of these places only really get going after midnight, but if you still have some energy, put on your best clothes and head for **La Paloma** (*Carrer Tigre 27; Thur–Sun 1800–2130 and 2330–0500*), a sumptuous Modernist dance-hall which opened in 1904. The seats are decked in red velvet and the band still churns out *paso dobles* to a mix of old-timers and young trendies.

Barcelona's city parks

The bulldozing of entire blocks of the Raval to create a boulevard through its centre is merely the latest in a series of urban renewal projects designed to transform Barcelona's historic neighbourhoods. The theme of much of the work has been to 'open the city to the sky', letting in natural light and transforming dark, cramped, narrow streets into airy open spaces.

During the 1980s and 1990s, a number of city parks were created – not parks in the conventional sense, with gardens and lawns, but 'urban spaces' featuring modern sculpture, industrial architecture and avant-garde design. The best known of these is **Parc Joan Miró** (*Metro: Espanya or Tarragona*), built on the site of an

old slaughterhouse which closed in 1979. A huge cement square is dominated by a phallic sculpture by Miró, *Dona i Ocell* ('Woman and bird'), which stands 22m (72ft) high in its own small pool. The sculpture, fashioned out of concrete and covered with broken ceramics, was Miró's last major work, completed shortly before his death in 1983. The art historian Robert Hughes has called it 'a moon calf dropped from Brobdingnag'; others' comments are cruder and less complimentary. In the lower section of the park, old men play bowls beneath the palm trees and children play on the swings, while the giant sculpture is silhouetted against a backdrop of skyscrapers on Carrer Tarragona.

Not far from here, **Parc de l'Espanya
Industrial** (*Metro: Sants-Estació*)
occupies the site of a former textile
factory. Designed by the Basque
architect Luis Peña Ganchegui and
completed in 1985, it features a lake,
concrete steps and several modern
sculptures, including the popular ***Drac de Sant Jordi*** ('St
George's Dragon'), used as a children's slide. However, the
most remarkable element is the series of ten sinister-looking
watchtowers standing guard over the park, giving it the
appearance of a concentration camp. Some of the factory
buildings are incorporated into the park, a feature also used
to great effect at **Parc del Clot** (*Metro: Clot or Glòries*),
built into a depression in the ground on the site of an old
railway shed.

Barri Gòtic

The oldest part of Barcelona, known as the Barri Gòtic ('Gothic Quarter'), has churches and palaces, shady squares and narrow streets containing some of Barcelona's most eccentric shops.

BARRI GÒTIC

Getting there: the most convenient Metro stations are Jaume I and Liceu. The Barri Gòtic can also be reached by a short walk from Plaça de Catalunya along the wide promenade of Avinguda Portal de l'Angel.

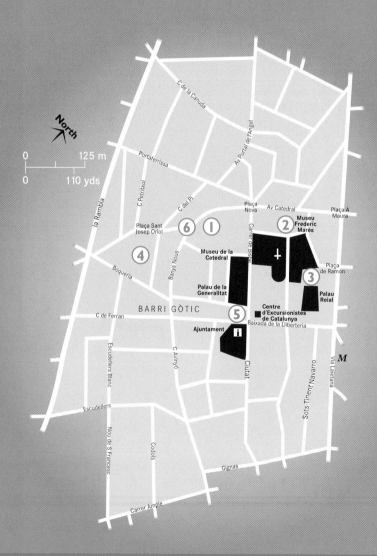

① Plaça de Sant Felip Neri

This pretty square, with its fountain and baroque church, sums up the whole appeal of the Gothic Quarter. Although it is situated close to the cathedral, it is hidden away down a narrow alley, and is therefore usually deserted. **Pages 52–3**

② Catedral

Barcelona's Gothic cathedral is dedicated to Santa Eulàlia, a 4th-century martyr and patron of the city who is believed to be buried in the crypt. A flock of white geese is kept in the cloister, possibly in order to reflect the purity of the virgin saint. **Pages 54–5**

③ Museu d'Història de la Ciutat

You can uncover the different layers of Barcelona's history at this extensive museum, as you explore the underground remains of the Roman city, visit the 14th-century royal chapel and climb to the top of a 16th-century watchtower. **Page 57**

④ Plaça del Pi

This charming square and its two close neighbours are lined with cafés and old-fashioned shops. Each of them makes a good place to sit out in the sun soaking up the bohemian atmosphere, especially at weekends when painters set up their stalls in the square. **Page 58**

⑤ Plaça Sant Jaume

The rival power bases of the city and Catalan governments face each other across this large square, a setting today for traditional Catalan festivities and the symbolic centre of the city in Roman times. **Page 59**

⑥ Barri Gòtic shops

The back streets of the Gothic Quarter are full of quirky, specialist shops, featuring everything from candles to carnival costumes, and feathers to fans. There are also several good art and antique shops in the lanes around the cathedral. **Page 61**

51

Tourist information

There is a tourist information office on the ground floor of the city hall on **Plaça Sant Jaume** (*open: Mon–Sat 1000–2000, Sun 1000–1400, closed 1 Jan and 25 Dec*). The main entrance is just around the corner on Carrer de la Ciutat.

Tip

The shops in the Barri Gòtic keep fairly conventional hours, so the area is best explored during the morning or early evening. For an introduction to the quarter, take one of the English-language walking tours which depart from the tourist office on Plaça de Catalunya. The tours start on Saturday and Sunday at 1000 and last about two hours. It is best to book in advance.

A stroll through the Barri Gòtic

The walk starts at Plaça de Catalunya and ends near the Jaume I Metro station.

The Barri Gòtic seems designed for strolling, and the best way to appreciate it is to wander from place to place, with certain aims in mind but with a willingness to be diverted by whatever catches your eye, whether it is a Gothic doorway, a pair of street musicians or a shop window filled with tempting sweets.

Start on Plaça de Catalunya and head down **Avinguda Portal de l'Angel**, a historic gateway to the city. This is now a busy pedestrian shopping street, dominated by fashion houses and a branch of **El Corte Inglés** featuring books, CDs and sports equipment. Among the quirkier shops to survive are **Planelles-Donat** (*No 25*), makers of *turrón* (Spanish nougat), and **Rosès** (*No 15*), which specialises in religious sculpture. Come here at Christmas time and the traditional crib decorations will include a *caganer* (literally 'shitter'), a portly figure of a shepherd relieving himself which is unique to Catalonia.

The avenue runs out close to **Plaça Nova**, where the brutal 1960s façade of the College of Architects is enlivened only by a frieze of a Picasso design. Across the square, a **section of Roman wall** still stands beside the cathedral, with the Gothic palace **Casa de l'Ardiaca**, now the city history archive, built on top. Walk down Carrer del Bisbe with the episcopal palace on your right until you come to the cathedral cloisters. In the small square facing the entrance, a monument commemorates the heroes of the resistance to Napoleon in 1809.

An alley leads to **Plaça de Sant Felip Neri**, built on the site of an old cemetery. This peaceful square is one of the most attractive in Barcelona, with a fountain at its centre

and a baroque church pockmarked with bullet-holes from the Civil War. The shoemakers' guild is situated here, its coat of arms on the façade of the building, and a small **shoe museum** (*see page 78*). Beyond are the dark streets of the **Call**, one of the leading centres of Jewish culture in Europe until it was destroyed in 1391.

The old synagogue on Carrer Sant Domènec del Call is now being restored and turned into a museum.

Return to Carrer del Bisbe and walk under the neo-Gothic bridge, designed by Gaudí's pupil Joan Rubió i Bellver in 1928. This leads into **Plaça Sant Jaume** (*see page 59*), seat of the Catalan government. Now take Carrer de Paradis from the square's northern corner to reach the **Centre d'Excursionistes de Catalunya**, whose courtyard contains four columns from the **Roman temple of Augustus**, built in the 1st century AD and rediscovered almost 2 000 years later.

53

> " *I began to haunt the old city. I could hardly wait for darkness to fall, when the lamps would be lit high up on the walls, and the streets would become shadowy, ghostly. This was the late medieval world of master craftsmen, stonecutters, masons and architects surviving intact in the middle of a city.* "

Colm Tóibín, *Homage to Barcelona*, 1990

Emerging behind the apse of the cathedral, bear right to reach Plaça del Rei, surrounded by the various buildings of the **Museu d'Història de la Ciutat** (*see page 57*). Now head down to Baixada de la Llibreteria, with its small, specialist shops. At the foot of the street, turn left to reach **Plaça de Ramon Berenguer el Gran**, dominated by an equestrian statue of Count Ramon Berenguer III. The view from here towards the old town is one of the best-known images of Barcelona, with Roman, Romanesque and Gothic features piled one on top of the other.

Catedral

Plaça de la Seu. Tel: 93 315 1554. Metro: Jaume I. Open: 0900–1300, 1600–1900 daily. Admission free. Museum open: 1030–1300 daily. £.

With an endless throng of visitors and little sense of peace, it is sometimes hard to remember that this is a sacred site, but Barcelona's cathedral has been at the centre of the city's life and worship for over 1 500 years. It is built on the remains of an early Christian basilica, parts of which survive in the **Museu d'Història de la Ciutat** (*see page 57*); when this was destroyed by the Moors in the 10th century, a Romanesque cathedral was put up in its place. The present building dates from 1298 and is a **fine example of Catalan Gothic art**, though the neo-Gothic façade was only added in the early 20th century.

With three naves of roughly equal width and an intricately carved wooden choir at the centre, the cathedral is typical of the Catalan Gothic style. In contrast to the simplicity of

Barcelona's other great Gothic church, Santa Maria del Mar (*see page 73*), it is filled with **richly decorated side chapels**, **Gothic altarpieces** and an abundance of **gold leaf**. Together with the choir, these lend it a dark, rather cluttered appearance and make it harder to appreciate the whole.

The cathedral is dedicated to **Santa Eulàlia**, a 4th-century Christian convert of legendary beauty and purity who was tortured and eventually put to death by the Roman rulers of Barcelona. Of the many torments which she is said to have suffered, one was to be rolled down the nearby Baixada de Santa

Eulàlia in a barrel perforated with knives. Her **alabaster tomb**, carved in Pisa in the 13th century, is kept in the crypt, situated directly beneath the main altar and reached by a staircase from the centre of the nave. On the feast of Santa Eulàlia (12 February), the people of Barcelona come to light candles and pay homage to the city's patron saint. Nearby, hanging on the wall to the right of the altar, are the painted wooden tombs of Count Ramon Berenguer I and his wife, who founded the second Romanesque cathedral on this site.

The **14th-century cloisters**, with their magnolia, palm and orange trees, are particularly attractive. A flock of

13 **white geese** is kept here and there are numerous explanations for this custom. Some say they are a reminder of the 13 torments suffered by Santa Eulàlia; that they reflect her age when she died; that they are a symbol of her virginity. Other sources claim that the geese have nothing to do with Santa Eulàlia at all, but were placed here as a reminder of the greatness of Barcelona in Roman times. Whatever the truth, they have become an indispensable part of the cloister, adding to the atmosphere if not the sense of tranquillity.

Look out, too, for the fountain with a **15th-century statue of St George**, as well as side chapels that once belonged to the medieval guilds. Look carefully at the floor and you will see the symbols of the guilds, such as scissors for tailors and a boot for shoemakers, carved into the stone. The cloisters also give access to the cathedral museum, which contains silver treasures and altarpieces by the Gothic painters **Jaume Huguet** and **Bernat Martorell**.

" *No matter how secure Barcelona felt, no matter how impregnable it was, its church architects obdurately kept the image of the fortress at the back of their minds.* "

Robert Hughes, *Barcelona*, 1992

Museu Frederic Marès

Plaça de Sant Iu. Tel: 93 310 5800. Metro: Jaume I. Open: Tue, Thu 1000–1700; Wed, Fri, Sat 1000–1900; Sun 1000–1500; closed Mon. £.

This utterly absorbing museum owes its existence to one man who had the foresight to realise that future generations would be fascinated by the ephemera of everyday life.

Frederic Marès (1893–1991) was a sculptor and an inveterate collector of everything from cigarette cards to mathematical instruments; when he donated his collection to the city, the museum was established in a section of the royal palace which once housed the tribunal of the Spanish Inquisition.

The first two floors are given over to a **large collection of sculptures**, from Iberian bronze figures dating back to the 6th century BC through to Roman marble and Gothic sacred art. When you tire of these, seek out the **Collector's Cabinet**, a series of themed display rooms featuring 19th-century objects. You could easily lose yourself here among the thousands of nativity figures, door-knockers, steam irons, cigar boxes, cameras, pocket watches and pipes. The **Ladies' Room** contains fans, gloves, necklaces and sewing machines; the **Gentlemen's Room** features snuff boxes, opera glasses and walking sticks. This leads into **Marès' study**, where he worked from 1952, which contains a collection of his sculptures as well as books and personal effects.

Save the best for last, and head for the top-floor **Entertainments Room**, where toy soldiers are found alongside penny-farthing bicycles, rocking horses, wind-up gramophones and games of bagatelle. Afterwards you can relax in the **Café d'Estiu** (*open: Apr–Sept only, Tue–Sun 1000–2200*), a delightful summer café in the grounds of the palace orchard which is shared with the neighbouring city history museum.

Museu d'Història de la Ciutat

Plaça del Rei. Tel: 93 315 1111. Metro: Jaume I. Open: June–Sept, Tue–Sat 1000–2000, Sun 1000–1400; Oct–May, Tue–Sat 1000–1400, 1600–2000, Sun 1000–1400; closed Mon. ££.

The beauty of Barcelona's history museum is that it allows you to delve into the city's multi-layered past and feel as though you are treading in the footsteps of past generations. It begins with an underground visit to **Roman Barcino**, where excavations have uncovered fascinating details of everyday life such as wine cellars, laundries and fish-salting factories. The remains extend as far as the cathedral, beneath which are various religious buildings including a **4th-century baptistery** and an **early Christian necropolis**.

The tour then leads into the former royal palace, where you can visit the throne room (**Saló del Tinell**) where Ferdinand and Isabella are said to have received Columbus on his return from America in 1492. Here, too, is the **14th-century chapel of Santa Àgata**, built directly on to the Roman wall. The chapel gives access to the **Torre del Rei Martí**, a 16th-century watchtower offering splendid views of the city. The ticket also includes a dramatic audio-visual show offering a 'virtual history' of Barcelona in several languages.

> *In the Middle Ages, without a natural harbour, Barcelona became the centre of a great maritime empire. In modern times, without iron or coal, she led Spain's industrial revolution.*
>
> **Felipe Fernández-Armesto,** *A History of Barcelona*, **1992**

The various parts of the museum are situated around **Plaça del Rei**, the city's most perfectly preserved Gothic ensemble. Ironically, it was only during the building of the nearby Via Laietana, which necessitated moving the medieval Casa Padellàs stone by stone to this site, that the remains of the Roman city were discovered. Such cultural vandalism would almost certainly not be allowed today.

Plaça del Pi

Metro: Liceu.

This pretty square just off La Rambla takes its name from the solitary pine at its centre. Shaded by orange trees and lined with cafés, this is one of the most pleasant spots in Barcelona for relaxing over a drink. In fact there are three squares – the others are Plaça Sant Josep Oriol and Placeta del Pi – grouped around the Gothic church of **Santa Maria del Pi**, but most people refer to them by a single name. The church itself was completed in the 15th century and is notable for its **massive rose window** and its **stained glass**, most of which had to be replaced following damage sustained during the Civil War.

The squares have a slightly bohemian atmosphere and are popular with artists, musicians and young travellers, who gather around the tiny **Bar del Pi** where the crowd spills out on to the square. Painters set up their stalls in Plaça Sant Josep Oriol at weekends, and there are so many buskers that the authorities have introduced restrictions in order to protect the local residents from unwanted noise.

Twice a month (*first and third Fri, Sat and Sun*), Plaça del Pi is home to a lively **food market** which features speciality products such as honey, farmhouse cheeses and handmade chocolate, and several of the best shopping streets in the Barri Gòtic radiate from here (*see page 61*). The squares themselves are also lined with interesting shops, from **Coses de Casa**, which sells traditional Catalan fabrics, and **Ganiveteria Roca**, specialising in knives, razors and scissors, to **Condoneria**, which features novelty condoms and rude toys.

Plaça Sant Jaume

Metro: Jaume I.

With rival centres of power facing each other across the square, Plaça Sant Jaume is a forceful symbol of the political divisions in modern Catalonia. Since the return of democracy in 1980, the Generalitat (Catalan government) has been controlled by the centre-right coalition of its president, Jordi Pujol, while the city of Barcelona, with its large immigrant and working-class population, has consistently voted in socialist administrations.

The president and the mayor have their own palaces, built around a Gothic core with later additions. The easier to visit is the Ajuntament (City Hall), which is open to the public on weekend mornings. The original Gothic entrance survives on Carrer de la Ciutat, while the neo-classical façade on Plaça Sant Jaume leads to a courtyard filled with sculptures by Catalan artists including Joan Miró, Josep Llimona and Josep Clarà. The highlight of the building is the Saló de Cent, a magnificent 14th-century council chamber bedecked with tapestries in the red and gold colours of the Catalan flag.

Across the square, the Palau de la Generalitat is generally open on the second and fourth Sunday of each month. Each year on 23 April, the doors are thrown open and the Gothic courtyard is filled with roses in honour of Catalonia's patron Sant Jordi (St George). There is a small figure of St George above the original Gothic entrance on Carrer del Bisbe, and another of the saint on horseback above the balcony of the main Renaissance façade. It was from this balcony that Josep Tarradellas, president of the Generalitat in exile, greeted his people on his return in 1977 with the words *Ja sóc aquí* ('I am here').

Tip

With its symbolic importance to the city, Plaça Sant Jaume has become a focal point for political demonstrations and for the revival of Catalan traditions and customs. Sardanas *are danced here on Sunday evenings, and at festival times the square is the setting for the building of human* castells *(*see page 62*).*

Restaurants

The main sights of the Gothic Quarter are located in its northern half, but in the evenings the focus shifts south. Many of the best restaurants and bars are found in La Mercè district, the lower half of the Barri Gòtic where it sweeps down to the sea.

Ateneu Gastronòmic

Pas de l'Ensenyança 2. Tel: 93 302 1198. ££. The 'gastronomic academy' turns out inventive Mediterranean cuisine with a distinct Portuguese influence at this restaurant behind the city hall. Try coriander and garlic soup followed by steak with myrtle, then pumpkin and chocolate fritters for dessert.

Can Culleretes

Carrer Quintana 5. Tel: 93 317 3022. ££. Barcelona's oldest restaurant was founded in 1786 and deservedly remains popular. The speciality here is seafood, but the menu also features Catalan meat dishes such as chicken with *samfaina* (a Catalan version of ratatouille) and *botifarra* (cured pork) sausage with beans.

El Pintor

Carrer Sant Honorat 7. Tel: 93 301 4065. ££. The best of the restaurants around the cathedral, this serves creative versions of Catalan market cuisine in a stylish old building with exposed bricks and wooden beams.

Los Caracoles

Carrer dels Escudellers 14. Tel: 93 302 3185. ££. This busy, traditional restaurant is best known for its snails and the spit-roast chicken, which you can watch being cooked out on the street. It is more popular with tourists than locals but is still worth a visit for its lively atmosphere and authentic Catalan cuisine.

Pitarra

Carrer d'Avinyó 56. Tel: 93 301 1647. ££. Game is the speciality at this award-winning restaurant in the up-and-coming nightlife district down by the port. The specialities include chamois with mango and wild boar in chocolate sauce.

Shopping

The Barri Gòtic is full of the sort of small, specialist shops that are largely dying out elsewhere. The fashion and chain stores can be found on Avinguda Portal de l'Angel, but south of here, especially in the narrow lanes between the cathedral and La Rambla, eccentricity takes over: Carrer Petritxol is known for its art galleries, Carrer de la Palla for its antique shops, and Carrer de la Boqueria is good for jewellery and ethnic crafts. Some of the oldest shops are found on Carrer Banys Nous, including **Arca de l'Avia** (*No 20*), which features period costumes, antique furniture and fans, **Germanes Garcia** (*No 15*) for basketware, and the celebrated **Casa Morelli** (*No 13; Mon–Fri 1730–2000*), where 'La Plumista' sells ostrich feathers stacked high in cardboard boxes – just the thing for a night at the opera.

Cereria Subira
Baixada de la Llibreteria 7. Barcelona's oldest shop was established in 1761 as a ladies' fashion store, but now sells beeswax candles. With tiled floors, balconies and elegant caryatids, this shop is worth a visit for the décor alone.

El Ingenio
Carrer de Rauric 6. A Barcelona institution, founded in 1838 and still turning out masks and carnival costumes from their workshop, as well as juggling balls and other magic tricks. There are free magic shows for children on Thursday evenings (*1600–1800*).

La Cubana
Carrer de la Boqueria 26. This 19th-century haberdashery has a wonderful array of scarves, shawls and fans as well as buttons and bows in banks of old wooden drawers.

La Manual Alpargatera
Carrer d'Avinyó 7. Rope-soled espadrilles are stacked floor to ceiling at this historic shoemaking workshop, which also sells basketware, panamas and straw hats.

Bars

Els Quatre Gats (Carrer Montsió 3) *is a Modernist landmark where* Picasso *used to meet his bohemian friends, including the artists Ramon Casas and Santiago Rusiñol. These days it appeals mostly to tourists, who drop in for a beer and to admire Casas' painting of himself and the original owner, Pere Romeu, on a tandem bike.* Irati *(Carrer Cardenal Casañas 7) is a heaving Basque tapas bar near Plaça del Pi, particularly lively during the early evening when the* pintxos *(titbits of ham, cheese or fish on pieces of bread) are laid out along the bar. For a taste of old Barcelona, head for Carrer de la Mercè down by the port, where several* tascas, *or sailors' taverns, sell fried sardines, Asturian cider and pungent Cabrales cheese. One of the best is La Plata (Carrer de la Mercè 28).*

Catalan festivals and traditions

The flourishing of Catalan culture since the demise of the Franco dictatorship has seen the revival of a number of traditional festivals, noisy and colourful affairs with music, dancing and pre-Christian rituals involving fire and mythical beasts.

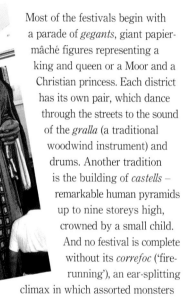

Most of the festivals begin with a parade of *gegants*, giant papier-mâché figures representing a king and queen or a Moor and a Christian princess. Each district has its own pair, which dance through the streets to the sound of the *gralla* (a traditional woodwind instrument) and drums. Another tradition is the building of *castells* – remarkable human pyramids up to nine storeys high, crowned by a small child. And no festival is complete without its *correfoc* ('fire-running'), an ear-splitting climax in which assorted monsters charge at the crowd while firecrackers explode around them in a haze of smoke.

All of this can be seen at the **Festes de La Mercè**, Barcelona's biggest festival, which begins on 24 September with an early-morning clarion call in the Barri Gòtic and continues for about a week. Almost as big is the **Festa de Santa Eulàlia**, which takes place on the nearest weekend to 12 February. Of the many neighbourhood festivals which

take place throughout Barcelona, the biggest is the **Festa Major de Gràcia**, held in the Gràcia district on or around 15 August. The **Festa de Sant Jordi** on 23 April commemorates the patron saint of Catalonia, St George. On this day, it is the custom for women to be given a rose and men to be given a book. Book and flower markets are set up on La Rambla, and a magnificent display of roses is held in the courtyard of the Palau de la Generalitat on Plaça Sant Jaume. Each of these has its origins in the *festa major* held in each Catalan town to mark the feast day of the patron saint.

One common feature of all Catalan festivals is the dancing of *sardanas*, traditionally performed by men and women holding hands alternately around a circle, accompanied by a *cobla*, an 11-piece band featuring clarinets, trumpets and a small wind instrument known as a *flabiol*. The *sardana* is above all a democratic dance, and anyone is welcome to join in. You can see *sardanas* every Sunday at 1200 in the cathedral square, and at 1900 in Plaça Sant Jaume.

" The sardana *is the most beautiful of all dances; it is a magnificent, moving ring.* "

Joan Maragall (1860–1911), *La Sardana*

El Born

The bars and clubs of the Born district are jumping well into the night in this most happening part of town, the place to go for Basque tapas, Brazilian cocktails and New Age vegetarian cuisine.

EL BORN

El Born

Getting there: the narrow lanes of the Born are not served by public transport, but most attractions are within a short walking distance of the Jaume I Metro station. Alternatively, you can enter from the seaward end by taking the Metro to Barceloneta or a bus to Pla del Palau.

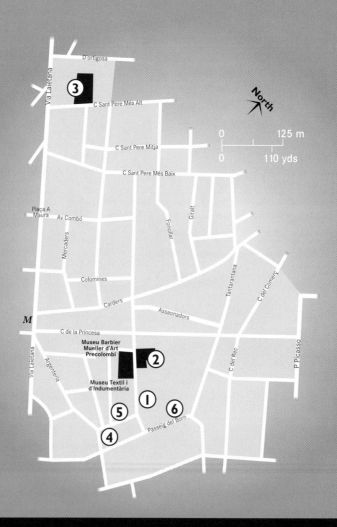

① Carrer de Montcada

Once home to wealthy merchants and aristocratic mansions, this medieval street is thriving once again, with palaces turned into art galleries, a string of interesting museums, and craftsmen at work in the nearby 'artists' quarter'. **Pages 68–9**

② Museu Picasso

It may not contain his best-known works, but the Picasso Museum, housed in a row of Gothic palaces, is still the biggest draw in Barcelona. It contains paintings and sketches from the artist's formative years, including his **Blue Period**, which he spent in Barcelona. **Pages 70–1**

③ Palau de la Música Catalana

Despite all the attention given to Gaudí, many people consider Domènech i Montaner's masterpiece to be the most perfect Modernist building in Barcelona. A concert here is an unforgettable experience. **Pages 72–3**

④ Santa Maria del Mar

This magnificent Gothic church with the dimensions of a cathedral dates from the time when the Born was the maritime trading district of the city. The beauty of the church lies in its simple lines and its overwhelming sense of space and light. **Page 73**

⑤ Casa Gispert

The aroma of coffee and roasted almonds hits you as you walk into this shop, more like an oriental bazaar with sacks of dried fruit and baskets of nuts strewn across the floor. Don't miss the **wood-roasting oven**, which has been in service since 1851. **Page 76**

⑥ El Born tapas trail

The latest craze to hit Barcelona is Basque *tapas* bars, where the *pintxos* are laid out along the bar for you to help yourself. A night-time tour of this district, with a few snacks here and there, makes an enjoyable if expensive substitute for an evening meal. **Page 74**

67

Tip

Avoid this area on Mondays, when all the museums are closed.

Carrer de Montcada

Metro: Jaume I.

The best-preserved medieval street in Barcelona was named after a noble family who took part in the 13th-century conquest of Mallorca. At one time this was the main street of La Ribera, an important mercantile trading quarter with links to the port district of Vilanova de la Mar. It was here that the rich merchants built their palaces, surrounded by the narrow lanes of the medieval souk, where the street names still reveal their origins as centres of trade: Assaonadors ('tanners'), Flassanders ('blanket-makers'), Sombrerers ('hat-makers'), Vidrieria ('glassmakers'), Argenteria ('silversmiths').

With the decline in Barcelona's maritime importance and the transfer of the port to the western side of the city, La Ribera fell into decay. Now, in one of those cyclical changes of fortune in which Barcelona seems to specialise, the district is on the way up again as the focus of waterfront activity shifts back towards the old port.

The street is lined with **handsome Gothic palaces**, with splendid courtyards and stone staircases leading to the main rooms. Many of these have been restored over the last 30 years to house museums, art galleries, cultural institutions and a school. The 15th-century **Palau Cervelló** is now **Galeria Maeght** (*No 25; open Tue–Sat 1000–1400, 1600–2000; admission free*), which showcases the work of some of the hottest contemporary artists. You can pick up an original Joan Miró lithograph here for a cool million or so pesetas, or an Antoni Tàpies for rather less. Across the street, the largely 17th-century **Palau Dalmases** is home to the classy cocktail bar **Espai Barroc** (*see page 77*).

Everyone comes here to see the Picasso Museum (*see pages 70–1*), but there are two other museums each of which rewards a half-hour exploration and can be visited on a combined ticket. The Museu Barbier-Mueller d'Art Precolombí (*No 14; open Tue–Sat 1000–2000, Sun 1000–1500; £*) is devoted to the ancient art of Spain's former Latin American colonies. It features Peruvian gold ornaments from the 3rd century BC along with sculptures, pottery and fertility objects from the Chupicuaro, Aztec and Mayan civilisations. The museum is located in the Palau Nadal, which dates back to the 15th century, when Spain's American expansion began. The shop here sells a good range of Latin American art and artefacts. In the adjoining Palau de los Marqueses de Llió, the Museu Textil i d'Indumentària (*No 12; open Tue–Sat 1000–2000, Sun 1000–1500; £*) features exhibitions of clothing and textiles, from 3rd-century Coptic cloth to Flemish tapestries, Chantilly lace, Regency dresses and Louis XV fans. It also houses the Manuel Rocamora collection of historic fashions, including chiffon and crêpe designs from the 1930s. Afterwards, you can relax with a drink in the courtyard café, a lovely spot at any time of day but especially at night when candles are put out on the tables.

The area around Carrer de Montcada has become known as Barcelona's 'artists' quarter', home to numerous art and craft workshops just as it was in medieval times (*see page 76*). Also of interest, at the lower end of Carrer de Montcada, is Passeig del Born, named after the jousting tournaments that were held here. This was once the setting for the burning of heretics by the Inquisition, but these days it is a popular night-time promenade lined with trendy cafés and bars.

" *A Basque joint, all roasted red and green peppers, fat olives, fresh salmon, lobster and prawn. I could not believe it the first time I went there. You stand there and help yourself to the range of delights on display … when you are ready to leave, the waiter asks you how many* tapas *you have had.* "

John Carlin, *Daily Telegraph*, 2000

Museu Picasso

Carrer de Montcada 15–19. Tel: 93 319 6310. Metro: Jaume I. Open: Tue–Sat 1000–2000; Sun 1000–1500; closed Mon. ££ (admission free on first Sun of each month).

The most visited museum in Barcelona was founded in 1963 in the 15th-century Palau Berenguer d'Aguilar but has gradually expanded to take over an entire row of Gothic palaces on Carrer de Montcada. It is devoted to **Pablo Picasso** (1881–1973), the Spanish painter who spent his formative years in Barcelona. His masterpieces may be elsewhere, in Paris, Madrid and New York, but the appeal of this museum lies mostly in the light it sheds on his early development, including his so-called Blue Period, which he spent in Barcelona.

Born in the Andalusian city of Málaga, Picasso moved to Barcelona at the age of 13 when his father was appointed

professor of fine arts at an academy in El Born. Apart from a brief spell in Paris between 1900 and 1902, he remained in Barcelona for nine years. It was here that he came into contact with the ideas of **Catalan Modernism**, meeting painters like Ramon Casas and Santiago Rusiñol in Els Quatre Gats café (*see page 61*) and establishing a lifelong friendship with his secretary **Jaume Sabartés**, who was later to found this museum. It was here, too, from a studio in Carrer Nou de la Rambla, that Picasso

EL BORN

had his first experiences of the low-life of El Raval that was to influence his Cubist classic ***Les Demoiselles d'Avignon***, set in a brothel on Carrer d'Avinyó and now exhibited in the Museum of Modern Art in New York.

Perhaps this is why the Catalans like to claim him as their own, as part of the 'holy trinity' of 20th-century Catalan artists with Miró and Dalí. Indeed, despite his roots, Picasso might have felt more Catalan than Spanish. Cut off from Spain throughout most of the Franco years, he remained close to Barcelona and donated much of his work to this museum, yet he always refused to allow his most famous and controversial painting, *Guernica*, to be exhibited in Spain while Franco was still alive.

The museum contains over 3 000 paintings, sketches and lithographs, together with ceramics donated by Picasso's widow, though only a small selection is on display at any one time. The collection is arranged chronologically, making it easy to follow Picasso's development from schoolboy drawings and landscapes of Barceloneta beach through experiments with Impressionism and then his Blue Period (1902–4). Inevitably, since the focus is on work produced in Barcelona, there are huge gaps: there is virtually nothing between 1904 and his *Harlequin* of 1917, donated to the city during a visit to his mother, and an even bigger leap takes you to *Las Meninas*, Picasso's interpretation of a series of Velázquez paintings, drawn in 1957 and later given to the museum in memory of Jaume Sabartés.

Despite the crowds, the museum is a delightful place to spend a couple of hours. The enjoyment is enhanced by the setting, with courtyards to stroll in when you need a break. One of the paintings, actually set in Madrid, depicts a street violinist. Listen carefully as you wander around and you will probably hear musicians playing in the street outside, just as they did when Picasso lived in Barcelona.

Palau de la Música Catalana

Carrer de Sant Francesc de Paula 2. Tel: 93 295 7200. Metro: Urquinaona. Open: 1000–1500 daily, except when performances are taking place. ↳↳. Box office open Mon–Sat 1000–2100 and one hour before performances on Sun.

Most visitors to Barcelona head straight for Gaudí's monuments in the Eixample; far fewer discover the most emblematic Modernist building of all, hidden away in the unfashionable Sant Pere district to the north of El Born. This lavish concert hall was designed in 1905 by **Lluís Domènech i Montaner** as the home of the Catalan choral society Orfeó Català. From the extravagant façade, rich in mosaics and floral columns, to the sumptuous main hall with its skylight dome, this building is **a classic example of the Catalan Modernist style**.

The only way to visit the interior is on one of the excellent guided tours, which take place every half-hour in Catalan, Spanish and English. The guides explain the symbolism of Montaner's architecture, from the repeated use of the Catalan flag, the rose and the figure of St George (all symbols of Catalan nationalism) to the deliberate incorporation of street lamps and balconies to provide a gradual transition from the street outside. Montaner had access to the best mosaic and stained-glass artists of his day, as well as sculptors including **Eusebi Arnau**, **Pau Gargallo** and **Miquel Blay**. Don't miss Blay's remarkable sculptural group on the façade, *La Cançó Popular Catalana*, with its references to Catalan folk traditions.

Also on the façade are Arnau's busts of Bach, Beethoven, Palestrina and Wagner, the message being that Catalan culture would sit comfortably with the classics. This is reinforced by sculptures to either side of the main stage, one featuring Wagner's Valkyries, the other alluding to the popular Catalan song *Les Flors de Maig* ('The Flowers of May'). This mix between high European culture and Catalan folk art is also reflected in the programme, which ranges from symphonies to jazz and choral concerts to *sardanas*.

If you can, get to a concert here – whatever the music. It was here in 1960 that Catalan nationalists sang their unofficial anthem during a concert for General Franco – leading to the imprisonment of the current Catalan president Jordi Pujol.

The entire building was sympathetically restored during the 1980s by the architect Oscar Tusquets, who is now working on an extension to the building on the site of a demolished church. In 1997, the palace was recognised as a supreme example of Modernist art when Unesco declared it a World Heritage Site.

Santa Maria del Mar

Plaça de Santa Maria. Tel: 93 310 2390. Metro: Jaume I. Open: 0900–1330, 1630–2000 daily. Admission free.

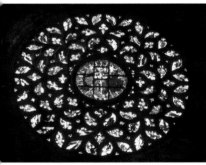

The triumph of Catalan Gothic architecture in Barcelona is this **magnificent church**, known as 'the people's cathedral' and a popular place to get married. Built between 1329 and 1384 at the height of La Ribera's maritime importance, the church has always been associated with fishermen and sailors.

Of several impressive pieces of stained glass, notice the **15th-century rose window** above the main door. The church was stripped of its choir and most of its interior decoration during the Civil War, allowing visitors to appreciate all the better the harmony of its simple lines, slim columns and **exceptional fan vaulting**, uncluttered by monuments and flooded with space and light.

<blockquote>
" O flag of Catalonia,
Our hearts keep faith with you.
You will fly like a brave bird
Above our desires. "
</blockquote>

Joan Maragall (1860–1911), *El Cant de la Senyera*, sung by Catalan nationalists during a visit by Franco to the Palau de la Música Catalana in 1960

Restaurants

Al Passatore
Pla del Palau 8. Tel: 93 319 7851. £.
This bustling Italian restaurant has a wide selection of wood-fired pizzas as well as fresh pasta dishes and a good-value set lunch.

Cal Pep
Plaça de les Olles 8. Tel: 93 310 7961. ££. The squid, prawns and anchovies are as fresh as they come at this lively seafood restaurant, where you sit at the bar watching owner Pep grilling the day's catch.

El Pebre Blau
Carrer Banys Vells 21. Tel: 93 319 1308. ££. Evenings only. This hip designer restaurant typifies the cosmopolitan nature of this area, offering new Mediterranean and Moroccan cuisine with Irish and Indian touches in a stylish, modern setting.

Gades
Carrer de l'Esparteria 10. Tel: 93 310 4455. ££. Evenings only. Carpaccios of salmon and ostrich followed by a cheese fondue with a plate of chips to share are among the specialities at this buzzing back-street restaurant.

La Flauta Mágica
Carrer Banys Vells 18. Tel: 93 268 4694. ££. Evenings only. Vegetarian cuisine takes on a post-modern look at this funky New Age restaurant, with more than a hint of Japanese influence. As well as rose-petal omelette and banana leaves stuffed with jasmine rice, there are also one or two organic meat choices.

Salero
Carrer del Rec 60. Tel: 93 319 8022. ££. The Japanese influence is clear in dishes like chicken teriyaki and *kakiage* (sautéed squid with courgettes and carrot) at this trendy Manhattan-style factory conversion of a tuna-salting warehouse.

The *tapas* trail

From 1900 to 2200 every evening the bars of the Born are full of people drinking txakoli *(a fizzy Basque white wine) and nibbling on* pintxos *before heading home for dinner. These bite-sized Basque snacks mostly consist of morsels of meat, fish or cheese on slices of bread, though the better bars also bring out hot snacks such as sausages, kebabs and salt-cod fritters. The* pintxos *are priced equally, and the usual etiquette is to help yourself and count up the number of cocktail sticks on your plate when the time comes to pay. The best place to try* pintxos *is* Euskal Etxea, *a popular Basque restaurant and cultural centre. Other good places are* Golfo de Bizkaia (Carrer Vidrieria 12), *La Taverna del Born* (Passeig del Born 27) *and* Sagardi (Carrer Basea 10).

Cafés and bars

Café Textil
Carrer de Montcada 12. This café in the courtyard of the Textile Museum makes a lovely place to while away time over a coffee and a pastry, or snacks ranging from sandwiches and salads to Middle Eastern *tapas*.

Estrella de Plata
Pla del Palau 9. This former fishermen's bar has moved upmarket and now serves 'designer *tapas*' such as hunks of salmon and *foie gras* in port. There is no menu, so point to what you want.

Euskal Etxea
Placeta Montcada 1. The original and best of the Basque *tapas* bars, this place is heaving every evening just after 1900 when the vast array of *pintxos* is laid out across the bar. Ask for a plate and a glass of *txakoli*, and get stuck in.

La Vinya del Senyor
Plaça Santa Maria 5. The view of Santa Maria del Mar is part of the attraction at this smart wine bar on the church square, which offers a great selection of wines by the glass accompanied by plates of anchovies and ham.

Pla de la Garsa
Carrer dels Assaonadors 13. Tel: 93 315 2413. ££. For solid Catalan food, it's hard to beat this welcoming bar, set in a former stables with tiles on the walls. The speciality is a plate of cold cuts and cheeses, and there is an excellent four-course lunch menu.

Va de Vi
Carrer Banys Vells 16. The wine vaults in the magnificent setting of a 16th-century Gothic palace make a great place to sip Cava by candlelight at the start or end of the evening.

Xampanyet
Carrer de Montcada 22. With its tiled walls and old wine barrels, this is the original champagne bar, though the speciality is cider, accompanied by anchovies or a *tortilla* omelette. This is a good place to start a bar crawl in this district before hitting the *tapas* trail.

Shopping

As well as the art galleries on Carrer de Montcada, look out for the 'artists' quarter' between here and Carrer de la Princesa, especially on *Carrer Esquirol*, *Carrer Vigatans* and *Carrer Banys Vells*. Numerous artists and craftspeople have their workshops here, including painters, designers, jewellers, potters, glassmakers and tailors. The serious money is spent on Carrer de Montcada, but look out too for *Kitsch* (Placeta de Montcada 10), with its playful papier-mâché designs.

Casa Gispert
Carrer dels Sombrerers 23. The wood-burning oven has been roasting almonds since 1851 at this wonderful delicatessen, one of Barcelona's most traditional shops. Spices are sold from old wooden drawers, and the aromas of coffee, chocolate, cinnamon and saffron hang in the air. Bottles of oil and vinegar line the shelves, and sacks of dried fruit on the floor lend it the air of an oriental bazaar.

El Rei de la Màgia
Carrer de la Princesa 11. Portraits of famous magicians hang on the walls at this old-fashioned magic shop, where the staff appear from behind a theatre curtain and everything is done with a certain sleight of hand.

Vidrieria Grau
Carrer Vidrieria 6. Founded in 1837, this is the last of the old-style glassmakers in a street once devoted to the trade. The shop has been in the same family for five generations and some of the dusty bottles and jars have probably been around almost as long.

Cheese and wine

Tot Formatge (Passeig del Born 13) is one of the best cheese shops in Barcelona, offering Idiazabal from the Basque country, Cabrales from Asturias and Roncal from the Catalan Pyrenees, as well as little-known Catalan farmhouse cheeses.
To accompany your cheese, *Vila Viniteca* (Carrer dels Agullers 7) sells a huge range of Catalan and Spanish wines.

Nightlife

The late-night scene is mostly concentrated around the central promenade, Passeig del Born, behind the church of Santa Maria del Mar. Fashions come and go, but a couple of old favourites are the Brazilian cocktail bars Berimbau *(*Passeig del Born 17*) and* Miramelindo *(*Passeig del Born 15*), both of which offer Latin jazz as well as potent* mojitos *(white rum, lime juice, sugar and mint) and* caipirinhas *(sugar-cane spirit, lime and sugar). For something completely different, try* Pas del Born *(*Carrer Calders 8*), a tiny back-street bar which is reviving the traditions of cabaret, with occasional variety shows and trapeze artists on a Saturday night.*

Espai Barroc

Carrer de Montcada 20. Tel: 93 310 0673. Open: Tue–Sat 2000–0200; Sun 1800–2200. Concerts: Sun 1900 (baroque music), Thu 2300 (opera). *The courtyard of a 17th-century palace leads to this 'baroque space' where you can enjoy a completely over-the-top experience, with fresh fruit and flowers, antique paintings and furniture, and concerts of opera and classical music by candlelight.*

Barcelona's other museums

Most visitors head for the Picasso Museum and the great art collections on Montjuïc, but Barcelona also has a number of small, eccentric museums devoted to a single subject.

Museu de l'Eròtica

Rambla 96. Tel: 93 318 9865; www.eroticamuseum.com. Metro: Liceu. Open: 1000–2400 daily. ££.

Situated at the top of a staircase that looks like the entrance to a bordello, this museum combines a serious approach to the study of sexual images in various cultures with rather more eye-catching pornography. The exhibits include erotic carvings from India, phallic symbols from Thailand and explicit drawings from the *Kama Sutra*, plus sex toys, girlie magazines and a tribute to the golden age of Barcelona's music-hall district in the Raval.

Museu del Calçat

Plaça de Sant Felip Neri 5. Tel: 93 301 4533. Metro: Jaume I or Liceu. Open: Tue–Sun 1100–1400. £.

Barcelona's shoe museum is housed in the Renaissance headquarters of the shoemakers' guild on one of the old town's most attractive and peaceful squares. The collection spans the city's history, from Roman sandals to present-day footwear in a variety of styles and shoes belonging to famous Catalans. Shoemaking has always been an important industry here, and this is not as dull as it sounds.

Museu Tauri

Gran Via de les Corts Catalanes 743. Tel: 93 245 5804. Metro: Monumental. Open: Apr–Sept, Mon–Sat 1030–1400, 1600–1900, Sun 1030–1300. £.

Bullfighting has never been as popular in Catalonia as in the rest of Spain, but this museum in the city's only surviving bullring has a collection of costumes, posters and memorabilia as well as a display on the career of **Manolete**, the legendary matador killed in the Catalan town of Lleida in 1947. The bullring itself is a fine Modernist construction of Moorish-style brick towers and ceramic-covered eggs, built in 1910.

Museu de Carrosses Fúnebres

Carrer Sancho de Avila 2. Tel: 93 487 1700. Metro: Marina. Open: 1000–1300, 1600–1800 daily. Admission free.

Hearses and funeral carriages may sound an unlikely subject for a museum, but this is deadly serious. Featuring horse-drawn carriages to modern cars, all used in genuine funerals, it is located inside the offices of the municipal funeral service. There is no sign on the street, so you have to go inside and ask for the museum.

> **"** The Catalans are neither French nor Spaniards, but distinct people, both in language, costume and habits. **"**
>
> **Richard Ford, *A Handbook for Travellers in Spain*, 1855**

The
waterfront

It used to be said that Barcelona turned its back on the sea, but the Olympics have changed all that, with new beaches, marinas and promenades reclaiming the waterfront as a vital leisure resource.

THE WATERFRONT

Getting there: the nearest Metro stations are Drassanes, Barceloneta and Ciutadella-Vila Olímpica. Most of the attractions in this chapter are connected by a waterfront walk, which begins by the Columbus monument at the foot of La Rambla and continues as far as the Olympic village.

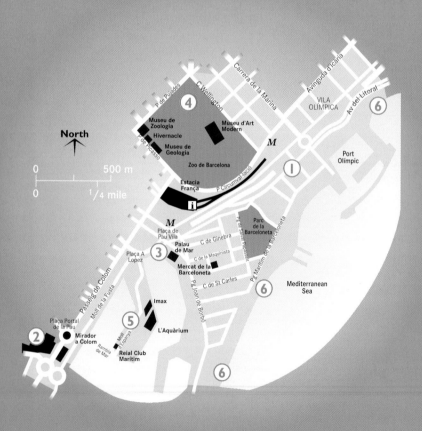

① Barceloneta

The old fishing village of Barceloneta has long been the place to come for a seafood lunch, and though it has lost much of its character it remains the best place for a huge platter of grilled fish or a *suquet* (fisherman's casserole). **Pages 84-5, 94-5**

② Museu Marítim

Catalonia's history as a major Mediterranean power is explored at this extensive museum, in the spectacular setting of the former royal shipyards. The highlight is a full-scale reproduction of the royal galley used at the battle of Lepanto. **Page 87**

③ Museu d'Història de Catalunya

This fascinating museum tells the story of Catalonia from the earliest settlers to the Franco dictatorship. History is brought alive through interactive exhibits and a series of imaginative reconstructions. **Pages 88-9**

④ Parc de la Ciutadella

Barcelona's largest park contains the Catalan parliament and an interesting modern art museum, but most people come here to stroll around the lake, picnic among the fountains or catch a glimpse of the world's only albino gorilla at the zoo. **Pages 90-1**

⑤ Port Vell

You can love it or hate it, but it is hard to ignore this huge modern development on the site of the old port. With waterfront *tapas* bars, an aquarium and a shopping mall which turns into a disco at night, this has quickly become one of the hottest spots in town. **Page 92**

⑥ Olympic port beach culture

The creation of new beaches to either side of the Olympic port has been a key factor in reorienting Barcelona towards the sea. On summer weekends the entire population of the city seems to be down by the Mediterranean, sunbathing on the beaches or strolling along the new beachfront promenade. **Page 93**

Tip

If you really want to look like a local, hire some rollerblades and head down to the waterfront promenade at weekends.

Barceloneta

Metro: Barceloneta. For restaurants, see pages 94–5.

Not long ago, tourists would come to Barceloneta for a splash of local colour, drawn by the fishing-village atmosphere and comparisons with the back streets of Naples and Marseille. These days they still come, to taste the seafood and stroll by the beach, but are disappointed to find that the Barceloneta of old is fast disappearing as the area becomes the centrepiece of the new, fashionable Barcelona-by-the-sea.

Built in the 18th century on a triangular spit of land, Barceloneta (whose name means 'little Barcelona') was the city's first housing estate, designed to rehouse those people displaced by the building of the citadel on what is now Parc de la Ciutadella. It soon became known as a place of sailors and fishermen, visited by the people of Barcelona for its **excellent fish restaurants** and *chiringuitos* ('kiosks') offering simple meals on the beach. The *chiringuitos* were torn down in 1991 because they did not fit in with the modern Olympic image the city wanted to create. At the time they were much lamented, and there was talk of Barceloneta losing its soul; now they have started to return, albeit in a more upmarket guise.

> *Fried baby eels arrived, like white spaghetti in boiling oil; raw goose-neck barnacles and steel platters crammed with six or eight kinds of grilled fish. The noisy room was full of families, three generations at each trestle table, from elderly patriarchs with seamed faces and nailbrush moustaches to allioli-smeared infants gumming their first squid.* **"**

Robert Hughes on the *chiringuitos* of Barceloneta, *Barcelona*, 1992

Fresh sand has been imported to improve the beaches, and at weekends the waterfront is crowded out with day-trippers, picnicking, strolling or rollerblading on the promenade. At the same time, just a few streets away, the old Barceloneta survives, with washing hanging from balconies in dark, narrow lanes, and bars around the market square selling fishy *tapas* and huge plates of prawns.

You can now walk the full length of Barceloneta's waterfront on an **attractive promenade**, which connects La Rambla and Port Vell with the Olympic port. It begins near the Palau de Mar, a converted depot with smart seafood restaurants and the **Museu d'Història de Catalunya** (*see pages 88–9*) at the start of Passeig Joan de Borbó. This boulevard, named after the father of King Juan Carlos, is perhaps the most striking example of the changes in Barceloneta's outlook. Until 1993 it was lined with warehouses; now it is open to the sea, with views across the harbour no one knew even existed. Again, there are numerous seafood restaurants with tables out on the pavement, not to mention waiters, who proffer menus in a generally vain attempt to entice you to stop.

At the end of this street, turn right past the fishing harbour (where a fish auction still takes place twice a day when the catch comes in) to stroll along the breakwater, or left for the long, straight **Passeig Marítim**, leading to the Olympic port. Along the way, you pass **Parc de la Barceloneta**, typical of Barcelona's new breed of urban parks, with a striking Modernist water-tower and a former gasometer incorporated into its design. As you walk along the beach, with skyscrapers looming up ahead, look out for Rebecca Horn's sculpture *Homage to Barceloneta*, placed on the site of the last *chiringuito* in 1992 in memory of a vanishing way of life.

Mirador a Colom

Plaça Portal de la Pau. Tel: 93 302 5224. Metro: Drassanes.
Open: Oct–May, Mon–Fri 1000–1330, 1530–1830, Sat–Sun 1000–1830;
June–Sept, 0900–2030 daily. £.

It may have been dismissed by Manuel Vázquez Montalbán as 'an outsize paperweight', but the monument to Christopher Columbus at the foot of La Rambla is a favourite image of Barcelona. Erected in 1888 at the start of the World Fair, this was a defining symbol of the new Barcelona that was showing itself off to the world.

Although Columbus had little to do with Barcelona, it was here that he was said to have been received on his return from the New World, when Ferdinand and Isabella bestowed on him the title of Admiral of the Ocean Sea. Such was the enthusiasm for Catalan nationalism at the time of the World Fair that there were even those who were ready to claim Columbus as Catalan. His figure stands atop the monument, pointing out to sea with his back turned towards Spain.

At 60m (197ft) tall, this is the largest monument of its type anywhere in the world. The base, with its **bronze lions** reminiscent of Nelson's Column in London, is frequently surrounded by scaffolding while repairs are carried out. Around the base are **stone sculptures** representing the medieval kingdoms of Spain, while the cast-iron column has capitals symbolising the four major continents of the world. You can take the lift up to the **viewing gallery** for the best views of the port, looking across the new marina and the houses of Barceloneta to the glistening skyscrapers of the Port Olímpic.

Museu Marítim

Avinguda de les Drassanes. Tel: 93 318 3245. Metro: Drassanes. Open: 1000–1900 daily. ££.

Barcelona's maritime museum is located in the magnificent setting of the **former royal shipyards**, built in the 13th century at the time of Catalonia's Mediterranean expansion to provide warships for the Catalan–Aragonese crown. This unique example of civil Gothic architecture, with its **cathedral-like arches and columns**, is worth a visit for the building alone. The exhibits cover the full range of Barcelona's seafaring history and include maps, navigational instruments, fishing boats and a collection of carved figureheads, as well as the story of Catalonia's Mediterranean conquests, which included the Balearics, Sicily and Sardinia.

> **"** *Barcelona had always been and continued to be a maritime city; it had lived off and for the sea; it was nourished by the sea, and gave back the fruit of its endeavours to the sea; the streets of Barcelona guided the wanderer's steps down to the sea, and that sea linked the city with the outside world.* **"**
>
> **Eduardo Mendoza,**
> ***City of Marvels**, 1986*

Pride of place goes to a full-scale reproduction of the **royal galley**, built here in 1568, in which Christian forces led by John of Austria defeated the Turks at the battle of Lepanto, a victory which marked a turning point in the fortunes of the various Mediterranean empires. The 60m (197ft) replica was built in 1971 on the 400th anniversary of the battle and gives a vivid picture of onboard life, with slaves chained to benches for 24 hours a day and surgeons, barbers, chaplains and musicians providing support for the crew. For a close-up look at the galley, you need to take the free audio-tour '**The Great Sea Adventure**', with an entertaining commentary featuring simulations on themes ranging from Spanish emigration to America to the invention of the submarine by the Catalan Narcís Monturiol.

Museu d'Història de Catalunya

Palau de Mar, Plaça de Pau Vila 3. Tel: 93 225 4700. Metro: Barceloneta.
Open: Tue–Sat 1000–1900; Sun 1000–1430; closed Mon. LL.

The museum of Catalan history opened in 1996 in a group of converted warehouses beside the old port. It is run by the Generalitat (Catalan government), so it should come as no surprise that history is tackled from a nationalist perspective. The main aim of the museum is to teach Catalans about their own history, so all captions are in Catalan – though a **helpful leaflet** which you can borrow from the main desk gives key dates and historical information in English.

The permanent exhibition, spread over two floors, explores Catalan history through a series of eight thematic displays, which are broadly arranged in chronological order. Each is enlivened by hands-on exhibits – you can tread an Arab water-wheel or try on medieval armour – which have led some critics to dub this a historical theme park.

The Roots looks at Catalonia's ancient history, using archaeological finds from the Iberian culture that thrived between the 6th and 2nd centuries BC and was the first on the Iberian peninsula to develop a written language. The **Roman and Arab conquests** of Catalonia are illustrated through reconstructions of Roman houses and an Arabic bazaar.

The Birth of a Nation deals with the origins of modern Catalonia, founded by Wilfred the Hairy around AD 878. It covers the feudal powers of the nobility and the church, the completion of the Reconquest, the building of the great Romanesque monasteries and the first written texts in Catalan.

Our Sea looks at Catalonia's **Mediterranean empire**, which began with the 13th-century conquest of

Mallorca and Valencia and extended over the next 200 years to include Sicily, Sardinia and Naples. The first Catalan literature appeared at this time and the first forms of parliamentary government were established.

On the Edge of the Empire deals with Catalonia's **period of decline**, following the unification of Spain under the Habsburg Austrian empire. There are tableaux depicting two events that are lodged in the Catalan memory: the revolt of *els segadors* ('the harvesters') against Spanish rule in 1640, and the loss of Barcelona during the War of Spanish Succession in 1714.

The Foundations of the Industrial Revolution and **Steam and Nation** look at the growth of the 18th and 19th centuries, with the arrival of railways, the expansion of Catalonia's cities and a flowering of Catalan nationalism and artistic expression which eventually produced the Modernist architectural movement.

The Electric Years deals with the early 20th century, a **period of political upheaval** that saw various forms of government set up and dismantled. This section culminates in the 1930s with the fall of the monarchy and the birth of the republic, followed by the Civil War and the execution of the Catalan president Lluís Companys.

Downfall and Recovery covers the **Franco dictatorship**, a disastrous period for Catalonia as its language, symbols and identity were ruthlessly suppressed. Popular culture is featured with a reproduction of a typical bar, and an account of the first days of mass tourism and the consumer society of the 1960s. The story ends with television coverage of Franco's funeral, followed by celebrations on the streets of Barcelona and the return of president-in-exile Josep Tarradellas.

" Perro Catalan, habla en cristiano
('Catalan dog, speak Christian') "

slogan aimed at Catalan speakers by fascist soldiers during the Franco régime

Parc de la Ciutadella

Metro: Arc de Triomf, Barceloneta or Jaume I. Open: 0800–2100 daily. Admission free.

The oldest, largest and greenest of all central Barcelona's parks is known by many people simply as 'the park'. Although it contains a handful of formal attractions, for most people this is a place to relax, stroll and picnic among the fountains, statues and ornamental gardens. Children come here in summer to row boats on the lake, lovers smooch on the benches and old men doze in the shade. It is where people go to escape the stresses of city life.

It was laid out in the 1870s on the site of the former citadel built by Felip V in 1715 following his successful siege of Barcelona. It was inevitable that one day the Catalans would pull down this hated fortress. Soon afterwards, the park became the central setting for the **1888 World Fair**, when the **Arc de Triomf** was built as the main exhibition entrance. This handsome triumphal arch, built of Moorish-style red brick with ceramic domes, is an **early example of Modernist art**.

The arsenal of the military citadel is now the Catalan parliament, which first met here in 1932 before being suppressed under Franco and restored in 1980. A wing of the parliament building houses the **Museu d'Art Modern** (*open: Tue–Sat 1000–1900, Sun 1000–1430; ££*), which features a selection of Catalan art from the 19th century to the 1940s. It begins with the works of the Romantic painter **Marià Fortuny** and the dark landscapes of the **Olot School**, then moves on to Modernism, represented by **Ramon Casas** and **Santiago Rusiñol**. If you have been to Els Quatre Gats (*see page 61*), you will recognise Casas' painting of himself and the owner, Pere Romeu, on a tandem, the original of which is displayed here. The museum also contains sculptures by **Josep Clarà**, one of the key exponents of *noucentisme*, a neo-classical reaction against Modernism. The influence of Rodin is clearly evident in his finely crafted nudes and classical expressions of female beauty.

" Gardens are to a city what lungs are to the human body. "
Josep Fontseré (1829–97), chief architect of Parc de la Ciutadella

Near here is the high point of the park, the **monumental fountain** designed by **Josep Fontseré**, in which the young Gaudi is thought to have had a hand. It is a triumphalist riot of angels, horses and figures from classical mythology, with water cascading down towards the lake. That other leading Modernist architect, **Montaner**, designed the café for the 1888 Exhibition which is now the **Museu de Zoologia** (*open: Tue–Sun 1000–1400, Thu to 1830; £*), filled with old-fashioned display cases of Iberian fauna. The building is better known as the Castell dels Tres Dragons ('Castle of the Three Dragons') after a popular play of the time. The nearby **Museu de Geologia** (*open: Tue–Sun 1000–1400, Thu to 1830; £*) is Barcelona's oldest museum, opened in 1882 to house the collection of minerals and fossils belonging to Francesc Martorell. Between the two is the delightful **Hivernacle**, a greenhouse built in 1884 which is now a café where concerts are occasionally held.

For many visitors, especially children, the highlight of the park is a visit to the **Zoo de Barcelona** (*open: May–Aug, 0930–1930 daily; Sept–Apr, 1000–dusk daily; £££*). There are dolphin shows, farm animals and an impressive collection of big cats, but the star attraction is undoubtedly Floquet de Neu ('Snowflake'), the world's only **albino gorilla** in captivity.

Port Vell

Metro: Barceloneta or Drassanes.

Port Vell ('the old port') is the epitome of the changes to Barcelona's waterfront. As recently as the 1980s, this

was a place of wharves and warehouses; now it has become the city's premier entertainment district. With a marina on the site of the old docks and a glistening new leisure centre on the quay, this area would be totally unrecognisable to anyone who had not seen it for 20 years.

The best approach is to walk across Rambla de Mar, an undulating wooden walkway at the foot of La Rambla which opened in 1994. This has become a busy promenade at all times of day, but especially during the early-evening *paseo* as people head for the *tapas* bars on the quay. Occasionally the bridge lifts up to allow a boat through and pedestrians have to wait, but that is all part of the fun.

The walkway leads to Moll d'Espanya, dominated by the huge Maremagnum complex. With 40 shops, restaurants and bars, and discos on the rooftop terrace, this place is buzzing day and night. There is also an eight-screen cinema and an IMAX multi-storey screen, between which you can find the Aquàrium (*tel: 93 221 7474, www.aquariumbcn.com; open: 0930–2100 daily, July and Aug to 2300; £££*), which claims to be the largest in Europe, with tanks containing seahorses and tropical fish and a walk-through glass tunnel where you can get close to sharks.

The two ends of Moll d'Espanya are joined by Moll de la Fusta, a palm-lined promenade on the site of the old timber wharf. When this opened in 1987, it was the first stage in Barcelona's cherished plan to open the city to the sea. The star attraction was Gambrinus, a designer bar by Xavier Mariscal with a sculpture of a giant crayfish on the roof. Today, the bar is abandoned, but the crayfish is still there, a symbol of a city that is forever reinventing itself.

Vila Olímpica

Metro: Ciutadella-Vila Olímpica.

Barcelona's successful Olympic bid triggered the development of this 'village' on industrial wasteland around the district of Poblenou. Built to house the athletes during the 1992 games, it was initially called Nova Icària after a utopian socialist community, but these days it is simply known as Vila Olímpica.

The centrepiece is the marina, **Port Olímpic**, which opened in 1988 and is surrounded by lively restaurants and bars. It is dominated by the twin towers of **Torre Mapfre** and **Hotel Arts**, which at 153m (502ft) are the tallest skyscrapers in Spain. Behind the Hotel Arts, Frank Gehry's golden *Fish* sculpture glistens in the sun, a symbol of post-Olympic Barcelona, which draws you ever closer as you walk along the beach.

> *Oh Barcelona, stop a moment: take a look*
> *At how the sea spreads blue towards the low horizon.*
> *Look at the little towns, sun-bleached, along the coast …*
> *And you want to flee from the sea?*
>
> **Joan Maragall (1860–1911)**

More than 4km (2 ½ miles) of new beaches have been created either side of the marina, making this one of the most pleasant spots in the city on summer afternoons. On **Bogatell beach** there are even a number of *chiringuitos*, stirring memories of the ambience of pre-Olympic Barceloneta. At weekends, when all of Barcelona heads for the sea, there are buskers and craft stalls on the waterfront; at other times, despite the parks, the promenade and the daring modern architecture, the 'village' has a rather desolate air, with few of the local shops and bars that characterise Barcelona's more genuine neighbourhoods.

Restaurants

For outdoor dining beside the sea, head for the fashionable seafood restaurants in the Palau de Mar or the more down-to-earth establishments along Passeig Joan de Borbó. Most of these are fine, but if the quality of the cooking matters more than the sea views, seek out some of the more traditional fish restaurants in the back streets.

Cal Pinxo
Carrer Baluard 124. Tel: 93 221 5028. ££. The best known of all Barceloneta's *chiringuitos*, patronised by writers and football stars, has been given a new lease of life beside the beach. Come here in summer to eat rice and fish dishes such as razor clams and grilled spiny lobster on a sunny beachside terrace.

Can Ramonet
Carrer Maquinista 17. Tel: 93 319 3064. ££. The oldest restaurant in Barceloneta was opened in 1763 and is still deservedly popular. You can eat outside on a charming market square, sit at wine barrels at the bar or splash out on black rice and grilled lobster in the restaurant at the back.

Can Ros
Carrer Almirall Aixada 7. Tel: 93 221 4579. ££. Hidden away behind the seafront promenade, this old-world dining-room with cubicles and wooden benches offers great-value seafood paella and fishy *tapas*. The five-course tasting menu features a selection of fried fish as well as seafood salad, stuffed peppers and salt cod with langoustines.

Can Solé
Carrer de Sant Carles 4. Tel: 93 221 5012. £££. This famous restaurant started out as a workers' tavern in 1903 and still preserves its original beer pumps and marble tables. The tourists tend to miss it as it is not on the seafront, but locals know it as one of the best places to eat in Barceloneta. As well as such dishes as black rice with *allioli* and salt cod with honey, this is reputed to be the birthplace of the Catalan fish stew known as *sarsuela* (seafood 'operetta').

Dzi
Passeig Joan de Borbó 76. Tel: 93 221 2182. ££. For something different, try this contemporary Asian restaurant situated close to Barceloneta's fishing port. Fresh local seafood is cooked in Chinese and Thai styles, or you can have meat dishes such as veal with mango.

El Rey de la Gamba
Passeig Joan de Borbó 46. Tel: 93 225 6400. ££. The 'King of the Prawn' occupies virtually an entire block of the harbourside promenade. You can share a large seafood platter for two, or order smaller portions of garlic prawns, oysters and live clams. There is another branch of this restaurant at the Port Olimpic.

Emperador

Palau de Mar. Tel: 93 221 0220. ££.
One of several fish restaurants lining
the waterfront in this renovated
warehouse, with terraces which take full
advantage of the afternoon sun. The
menu is more tourist-friendly than in
some of the more traditional Barceloneta
establishments, featuring steamed
mussels, paellas and a mixed seafood
grill as well as steak with green
pepper or Roquefort.

Salamanca Silvestre

*Carrer Almirall Cervera 34. Tel: 93
221 5033. ££.* This lively seafront
establishment brings back the
atmosphere of the *chiringuitos* with its
outdoor dining area facing the beach.
The emphasis is on seafood, but there
are also meat dishes such as Castilian-
style roast piglet, as well as plates of
ham and other *tapas* at the bar.

Suquet de l'Almirall

*Passeig Joan de Borbó 65. Tel: 93
221 6233. £££.* One of the best of
the seafood restaurants along the
promenade, with a handful of tables
out in the sun. The specialities are
paella in various styles, *suquet* fish
casserole and a *pica-pica* of fish dishes.
Those who prefer meat can have *foie
gras* in sherry.

Reial Club Marítim de Barcelona

*Port Vell. Moll d'Espanya. Tel: 93 310
5143. £££.* Barcelona's yacht club
turns its back on Maremagnum with
a terrace overlooking the marina and
the city beyond. The menu features
sophisticated fish dishes, such as
carpaccio of salmon with wasabi
(Japanese horseradish) or roast sea-
bream with rosemary and lemon.

Set Portes

*Port Vell. Passeig d'Isabel II 14. Tel: 93
319 3033. ££.* This venerable restaurant
was founded in 1836 and was the first
establishment in Barcelona to have
gaslights and running water. Che
Guevara, Federico García Lorca and
Joan Miró are among those to have
eaten here and enthused about its tiled
floor, white-clad waiters, 'blind man's
paella' (without bones) and traditional
Catalan cuisine.

Agua

*Vila Olímpica. Passeig Marítim de la
Barceloneta 30. Tel: 93 225 1272.
££.* Reached via a staircase from the
promenade and with tables right on
the beach, this makes a perfect setting
for an al-fresco meal. The menu
combines fresh seafood and traditional
rice dishes with creative versions of
modern Catalan cuisine.

El Cangrejo Loco

*Vila Olímpica. Moll de Gregal 29. Tel:
93 221 0533. £££.* The Olympic port
is lined with smart seafood restaurants
and this is one of the best, offering
top-notch versions of paella and black
rice as well as monkfish casserole and
salmon in orange sauce. Choose between
the upstairs restaurant overlooking the
beach, or tables downstairs beside
the harbour.

Lungomare

*Vila Olímpica. Carrer de Marina 16.
Tel: 93 221 0428. ££.* Situated at the
back of the Mapfre skyscraper and
overlooking the Olympic port, this
restaurant has some of the best Italian
seafood cooking in Barcelona, such as
grilled cockles with olive oil, pasta
with clams, or grilled hake with wild
mushroom risotto.

San Fermin

*Vila Olímpica. Moll de Gregal 22.
Tel: 93 221 0543. ££.* If you want a
change from seafood, this rustic-style
restaurant beside the Olympic harbour
offers a taste of the Basque country,
with cider poured from huge barrels
and T-bone steaks cooked on an
outdoor grill.

Nightlife

Since the opening up of the waterfront, the focus of after-dark activity has shifted increasingly down to the port, with numerous bars, clubs and discos in and around the Port Olímpic offering everything from techno and house music to designer tapas *and* nuevo flamenco. *The fashions here change so quickly that the only thing to do is to arrive after midnight, wander around and find something that appeals. Meanwhile, a young crowd gathers every night, and especially on summer weekends, at the discos on the top floor of the Maremagnum complex, of which* Nayandei *is the biggest and best known. Three clubs and a mock-Irish pub are gathered around an all-night mini-golf terrace, while on the lower levels Latin bars such as* Trocito *and* Mojito Bar *offer salsa and Cuban cocktails.*

Tapas-by-the-sea

Tapasbar, at the entrance to Maremagnum, features a great range of tapas *on a sunny waterfront terrace. This is just the place for a plate of* pa amb tomàquet, *an assortment of Catalan sausages, some spicy Galician peppers and a cold beer. There are also special tasting menus with a selection of* tapas *for two to share. There is another branch at the Port Olímpic, but without the outdoor tables or sea views. Beyond the Port Olímpic, the chiringuitos on Bogatell beach are bringing back the atmosphere of the Barceloneta of old. At Catamaran and Xiringuito Escriba, you can go inside for a full meal if you wish – but the real point is to sit out of doors beside the beach, nibbling on plates of fishy* tapas *such as steamed mussels, grilled prawns or baby squids cooked in their own ink.*

Shopping

Mercat de la Barceloneta

*Housed in an 1882 market hall between Carrer
Maquinista and Carrer Andrea Dòria, the market
(open: Mon–Sat 0900–1400, Fri 1630–2000) has
several good fresh fish stalls. The fishmongers
here buy much of their produce from the twice-
daily fish auction, which takes place on the
fishing harbour at the end of Carrer de l'Escar
in early morning and late afternoon.*

Boat trips

In 1888, as Barcelona celebrated the World Fair and the opening of the Columbus monument, the boat company Las Golondrinas began offering pleasure cruises around the harbour. Despite Barcelona's importance as a working port, the everyday life of the city was almost totally cut off from the sea, and these golondrinas *('swallow-boats') provided a rare opportunity for the citizens to get out into the fresh sea air, hear the seagulls and breathe in the salty tang of the sea. More than a century later, a ride on the* golondrinas *is still an essential Barcelona experience.*

❝ *We want to recuperate the centre without gentrification taking place, which is something other cities have not been able to achieve.* ❞
Joan Fuster, Barcelona city councillor, *The Independent***, 1999**

THE WATERFRONT

These days there are two basic options. The first is a short cruise on one of the traditional wooden boats. These boats are open to the elements, so there is little protection from sun, wind or rain. Throughout the summer and on winter weekends, they make regular round trips to the *rompeolas*, or breakwater, at the entrance to the inner harbour. The trip lasts about 40 minutes and you can either complete it in one go or disembark at the breakwater, where you can go fishing, have lunch or walk along the sea walls. On a good day, there is an enjoyable walk back to the city, passing Sant Sebastià beach and the fishing port of Barceloneta. If you want to return by boat, remember to check the times when you disembark.

The second option is to take a one-hour cruise on the modern Trimar catamaran, which has an open upper deck and a lower deck that is completely enclosed. This is certainly more comfortable, but not as much fun. The advantage is that as this is a sea-going vessel, it is able to take a much longer tour of the port area, continuing beyond the inner harbour and past Barceloneta to the Olympic port and the new beaches. A cruise on this boat is a good way to get an overall view of the changes that have taken place on Barcelona's waterfront in the last 20 years.

Getting there: Both boats depart from the jetty at Plaça Portal de la Pau, near the Columbus monument. They operate several times a day in summer and less frequently in winter. Tel: 93 442 3106.

Montjuïc

The green hill overlooking Barcelona
has long been a place of recreation,
where people would come to escape
the stifling heat and spend a day
enjoying the gardens and museums.

MONTJUÏC

*Getting there: bus 50 stops in Plaça d'Espanya and
continues up to Montjuïc, giving access to all the main
sights. A more enjoyable way of getting there is to take
the Metro to Espanya and walk down Avinguda Maria
Cristina before ascending to Montjuïc on the outdoor
escalators. In summer there is also a 'tourist train' with
regular departures from Plaça d'Espanya. Another alternative
is to take the Metro to Paral.lel and then the funicular to
Montjuïc, which connects with the Telefèric cable-car
to the castle.*

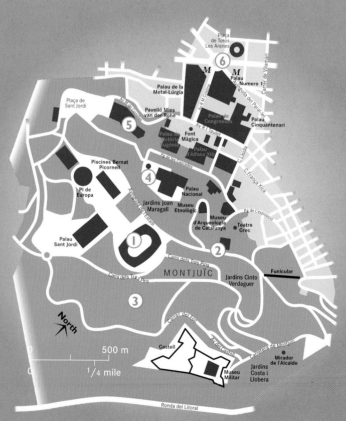

MONTJUÏC

① Estadi Olímpic

It may just look like a sports stadium, but the centrepiece of the 1992 Olympics has enormous symbolic value to Barcelona. It was the Olympics that put Barcelona on the map and provided the impetus for its reinvention as a city of culture and style. **Pages 104–5**

② Fundació Joan Miró

The colourful designs of Joan Miró are everywhere in Barcelona, from public sculptures to T-shirts and even the tourist board logo. This museum contains many of Miró's paintings and sculptures, instantly recognisable by their trademark symbols and use of primary colours. **Pages 106–7**

③ Jardí Botànic

The botanical garden on the city's former rubbish tip forms part of an ambitious plan to create a green belt across Montjuïc. There are many other parks and gardens scattered across the mountain, named after Catalan poets and a German environmentalist. **Page 108**

④ Museu Nacional d'Art de Catalunya

The glory of Catalonia's art museum is an outstanding collection of Romanesque murals, recovered from remote Pyrenean churches. The museum is housed in the Palau Nacional, the main building of the 1929 International Exhibition. **Pages 110–11**

⑤ Poble Espanyol

Another legacy of the 1929 Exhibition is the 'Spanish Village', with reproductions of traditional architecture from the various Spanish regions. Among the highlights are Andalusian patios, a main square modelled on Segovia and a complete Catalan Romanesque monastery. **Pages 112–13**

⑥ Plaça d'Espanya

This monumental square forms the classic entrance to Montjuïc, through an avenue flanked by Venetian-style towers. On summer evenings the illuminated fountains are the centrepiece of a spectacular sound-and-light show. **Pages 114–15**

Tip

There are good museum cafés in MNAC and Fundació Joan Miró, and a wide choice of restaurants at the Poble Espanyol, but otherwise there are few dining options on Montjuïc. One exception is Park-Montjuich (Avinguda de Miramar; tel: 93 441 4232) near the funicular station, which offers decent if somewhat pricey versions of traditional Catalan cuisine. It is often packed out with tour groups, so you need to arrive early if you want a table by the picture windows, which offer spectacular views.

Anella Olímpica

Bus: 50.

Considering how Barcelona promotes itself as an up-to-the-minute, style-conscious city, it is surprising how much capital it still makes out of an event that happened nearly a decade ago. The Olympic Games of 1992 played a huge part in boosting tourism and putting Catalonia on the world map, but by now you would have thought it was time to move on. The fact that the Olympic stadium is still one of Barcelona's biggest draws says as much about the iconic status of the games as it does about the stadium itself.

The main sights are grouped together around an 'Olympic Ring', which takes an hour or so to explore. Most people start at the **Estadi Olímpic** (*open 1000–1800 daily; admission free*), built for the International Exhibition of 1929 and extensively remodelled for the games. The original façade has been kept, with equestrian statues by **Pau Gargallo**, but the stadium has been expanded to hold some 60,000 spectators. A plaque beside the main gate pays tribute to **Lluís Companys**, the president of the Generalitat in 1936 who was responsible for organising a 'People's Olympiad' in opposition to the official Olympics in Nazi Berlin. Because of the Civil War, the

> " *Barcelona!*
> *It was the first time that we met*
> *Barcelona!*
> *How can I forget*
> *The moment that you stepped*
> *into the room*
> *You took my breath away.* "

Freddie Mercury and Mike Moran, *Barcelona* – recorded by Freddie Mercury and Montserrat Caballé as the anthem of the 1992 Olympics

games never took place, and Companys was executed on Franco's orders in 1940. The stadium is now the home of Barcelona's second football team, RCD Espanyol.

A promenade leads around the outside of the stadium to the Galeria Olímpica (*open: Mon–Fri 1000–1300, 1600–1800, Sat–Sun 1000–1400, extended hours in summer; £*), a museum with souvenirs and film footage of the 1992 games. Near here is Palau Sant Jordi, an indoor sports hall where the gymnastics events took place. Designed by Japanese architect Arata Isozaki, this is widely considered the most attractive of the Olympic installations. Outside the building, metallic sculptures of trees by Isozaki's wife Aiko Miyawaki lend a futuristic effect. From here you can walk down past the Piscines Bernat Picornell (the Olympic swimming pool) to Plaça de Europa, a magnificent vantage point dominated by Santiago Calatrava's space-age telecommunications tower. The complex is completed by Ricard Bofill's neo-classical sports university, the first major work in Barcelona by this controversial Catalan architect.

Castell de Montjuïc

Access by Telefèric (cable-car) from funicular station.

Unless you go by the cable-car (*closed on winter weekdays*), it is a stiff hike to reach this castle, but the reward is one of the best views in Barcelona. From the castle walls, you look down the steep grassy slopes of the former Jewish cemetery to the busy container port, a reminder of pre-Olympic, industrial Barcelona and its close links to the sea.

There are records of a fortress here since 1640, but the present building dates from the 18th century, designed as a star-shaped pentagon according to the French military model. For many years the castle was a hated symbol of repression; during the Civil War it served as a military prison, and it was here that President Lluís Companys was executed in 1940. The army handed the castle over to the city in 1960 and it now houses the Museu Militar (*open: Tue–Sun 0930–1930; £*), with collections of uniforms, weapons and Barcelona's only surviving statue of General Franco, removed from the parade-ground following the dictator's death.

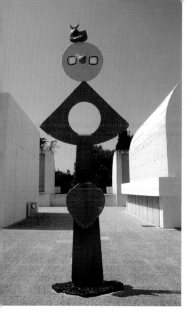

Fundació Joan Miró

Plaça Neptú. Tel: 93 329 1908;
www.bcn.fjmiro.es. Bus: 50. Open: Tue, Wed,
Fri, Sat 1000–1900; Thur 1000–2130; Sun
1030–1430; closed Mon. ££.

One of the greatest artists of the 20th century was born in Barcelona and has become indelibly linked to the city. The son of a Catalan watchmaker, Joan Miró (1893–1983) has sometimes been described as 'more surrealist than the surrealists', but what most people remember are his childlike spontaneity, playful sense of humour and use of bright primary colours – qualities which fit in well with Barcelona's modern image. Even if you know nothing about modern art, you will have seen some Miró in Barcelona: his mural at the airport, his pavement on La Rambla, his giant sculpture in the park that bears his name. The art critic Robert Hughes has gone so far as to call Miró the greatest artist Catalonia has produced since the 12th century.

The foundation was established by Miró himself in 1971, in a building designed by his friend Josep Lluís Sert. The bright, white walls and use of natural light lend the building a distinct Mediterranean feel and also take advantage of its setting overlooking the city. The collection includes paintings and sculptures donated by Miró and others given by his wife Pilar Juncosa and dealer Joan Prats. There are more sculptures in the garden and on the rooftop terrace, and the celebrated bronze and cement figure *Moon, Sun and Star* sits in its own small pool on the patio.

The collection allows you to trace the development of Miró's work, from the youthful realism of *Portrait of a Young Girl* (1919) to experiments with surrealism such as *Man and*

> **❝** *When I pick up a rock, it's a rock; when Miró picks it up, it's a Miró.* **❞**
> **Joan Prats, hatmaker, friend and patron of Joan Miró**

Woman in Front of a Pile of Excrement (1935), which has elements of Salvador Dalí about it. At around this time, Miró was deeply affected by the suffering of Catalonia during the Civil War, and his series of black-and-white lithographs, *Barcelona* (1939–44), reflects the darkness of the period. His later preoccupations, notably stars, moon, women and birds, are starting to emerge in *Morning Star* (1940) and *Woman and Bird in the Night* (1945), but are given full expression and a vivid sense of colour in the large canvases which he produced in the 1960s, such as *Catalan Peasant by Moonlight*, *Woman in the Night* and *Figure before the Sun*. His playfulness is even more evident in a **monumental tapestry**, designed for this space and best admired from an upstairs gallery, featuring stars, the moon and a vaguely half-human, half-animal figure.

The museum ends with *Homage a Miró*, a selection of works by other artists donated in Miró's memory. Among the artists represented are **Henri Matisse**, **Henry Moore**, **Eduardo Chillida**, **Richard Serra** and **Antoni Tàpies**, as well as the American sculptor **Alexander Calder**, who was a close friend of Miró's. The museum also contains Calder's *Mercury Fountain*, designed for the Spanish republican government's pavilion at the 1937 Exposition in Paris, the same exhibition at which Picasso's *Guernica* was first shown. Like *Guernica*, this was a tribute to a town that had suffered at the hands of the nationalists – in this case the mercury-mining town of Almadén, destroyed by Franco's troops during the Civil War.

Jardí Botànic

Parc del Migdia, Carrer del Dr Font i Quer. Tel: 93 426 4935. Bus: 50. Open: Mon–Sat 1000–1700 (1000–2000 in summer); Sun 1000–1500. £.

One of the pleasures of an outing to Montjuïc is the opportunity it offers for walking in the shade, among palm, pine and cedar trees and gardens filled with fountains and statuary. Until recently, the wilder southern slopes have been relatively undeveloped, but the opening of this botanical garden on a former landfill site in 1999 marked the beginning of an ambitious plan to create a green belt across the mountain. The garden, overlooking the Olympic stadium, features numerous species from those regions of the world which share a Mediterranean climate. There are now plans to develop a second garden on the site of the old funfair, which closed in 1999.

There are many other parks and gardens on Montjuïc, some named after Catalan poets and one after the late German environmentalist Petra Kelly. Any of these make a delightful stroll, especially Jardins Joan Maragall behind the Palau Nacional, with its ornamental fountains and avenue of magnolias; Jardins Cinto Verdaguer, above the funicular station, with its spring bulbs; and Jardins Costa i Llobera, with its astonishing varieties of cactus, tumbling down the hillside towards the port. Just above here, facing the old entrance to the amusement park, is the Mirador de l'Alcalde, a lookout point designed for the mayor of Barcelona, with views out to sea, a collage of pottery and broken bottles, and a modern sculpture, *Homage to Barcelona*, by Josep Subirachs.

Tip

The word 'Montjuïc' means 'mountain of the Jews' and derives from the fact that there used to be a Jewish cemetery here – though the name may also have its origins in Roman times, when it was known as the 'mountain of Jupiter'.

Museu d'Arqueologia de Catalunya

Passeig de Santa Madrona 39. Tel: 93 424 6577; www.mac.es. Metro: Espanya or Poble Sec. Bus: 55. Open: Tue–Sat 0930–1900; Sun 1000–1430; closed Mon. £.

This fairly dry museum, with explanations in Catalan and Spanish only, is nevertheless fascinating for anyone with an interest in **ancient history**. Housed in a neo-Renaissance pavilion built for the 1929 Exhibition, it contains archaeological discoveries from Catalonia and elsewhere which trace the human history of Spain from the earliest cave-dwellers to Iberians, Greeks and Romans. There are extensive finds from the Greek settlement at Empúries, as well as Etruscan vases, Iberian funerary objects and Carthaginian carvings from Ibiza. A highlight of the visit is the chance to walk across an **original Roman mosaic floor**. If this gives you a taste for archaeology, there are outposts of the museum in Girona (*see page 153*) and Tarragona (*see pages 160–1*) as well as at Empúries and the Iberian settlement at Ullastret.

Across the street from the museum, the **Teatre Grec** is a Greek-style open-air theatre built in a former quarry for the 1929 Exhibition, now the venue for a popular summer festival (*box office: Palau de la Virreina, Rambla 99; programme available in advance on www.grec.bcn.es*). You can climb up through the gardens of the theatre to reach the Fundació Joan Miró.

Museu Etnològic

Passeig de Santa Madrona. Tel: 93 424 6807. Metro: Espanya or Poble Sec. Bus: 55. Open: Tue, Thu 1000–1900; Wed and Fri–Sun 1000–1400; closed Mon. £.

The least known of Montjuïc's museums has a large permanent collection but only a small amount is on display at any time. The holdings include **Aztec pottery** and other **pre-Colombian artefacts**, as well as a number of items relating to Japanese popular culture in recognition of Catalonia's growing economic links with Japan.

Museu Nacional d'Art de Catalunya

Palau Nacional. Tel: 93 622 0360; www.mnac.es. Metro: Espanya. Open: Tue–Sat 1000–1900, Sun 1000–1430, closed Mon. ££.

Barcelona's only world-class museum collection is housed in a mock-baroque palace built for the 1929 International Exhibition. The Palau Nacional was conceived by the Modernist architect **Josep Puig i Cadafalch** as the spectacular central element of the vista to Montjuïc, and the best way to approach it is still from Plaça d'Espanya, on the outdoor escalators which emerge near the museum entrance.

> *Grave, austere, magnificent, erupting with emotion.* "
>
> **Adam Hopkins on Catalonia's Romanesque art, *Spanish Journeys*, 1992**

The main attraction of the museum is its collection of **Romanesque frescos**, unrivalled anywhere in Europe. Until the 19th century, Romanesque art was largely ignored, considered naïve and unsophisticated in comparison with the Gothic and Renaissance periods that followed. It was only when collectors began to strip bare the remote Pyrenean churches, established along the pilgrim route to Santiago in the 11th and 12th centuries, that Catalonia woke up to the loss of its heritage. Between 1919 and 1923 a concerted effort was made to seek out abandoned churches and recover their frescos, removing them whole and transporting them to Barcelona.

The frescos date from a time when literacy was still uncommon and pictures had to be used as a 'poor man's bible' to instruct Pyrenean villagers in the faith. They are remarkable for their simple, childlike images and vivid colours, as if they had been drawn by a 12th-century Joan Miró. Especially notable are the frescos from the church of **Sant Climent de Taüll**, consecrated in 1123, with a figure of the Pantocrator (Christ in Majesty) in the central apse. Like many of these frescos, it is displayed inside a reconstruction of the original church, with a photo and scale model to help you put it into context.

The museum's second major collection is of **Catalan Gothic art**, spanning the period of Catalonia's Mediterranean expansion and showing the Flemish and Italian influences

that came to the fore as a result. It begins with the murals from the **Palau Caldes** (now part of the Museu Picasso) depicting the conquest of Mallorca in 1229. The major Catalan artists of the period are represented, including **Ferrer Bassa** and **Lluís Borrassa**, whose painting of a young man leaning out of a window watching St Peter's crucifixion was taken from Barcelona Cathedral. There are altarpieces by **Bernat Martorell** and **Jaume Huguet**, and a fascinating gallery devoted to religious paintings in which an image of the donor appeared in prayer – a genre from which the art of portrait painting is thought to have developed.

The museum concludes with the **Cambó bequest**, a collection of Renaissance and baroque art donated by the financier Francesc Cambó. Although this occupies only a couple of small galleries, it includes works by many leading European artists of the 16th to 18th centuries, among them **Rubens**, **Tintoretto**, **Velázquez**, **Goya**, **Fragonard**, **Gainsborough** and **Tiepolo**. There are long-term plans to expand the collection, possibly incorporating the holdings of the Museu d'Art Modern (*see page 90*) to create a truly national art museum spanning the last thousand years.

The museum café serves coffee and snacks, as well as grilled meat dishes at lunchtime. It is situated in a corner of the **Sala Oval**, the grand central domed hall where concerts are sometimes held. Afterwards, remember to take in the view from the front terrace, looking down over Plaça d'Espanya and up to the mountain of Tibidabo in the distance.

Poble Espanyol

Avinguda del Marquès de Comillas. Tel: 93 325 7866; www.poble espanyol.com. Metro: Espanya. Bus: 50. Open: Mon 0900–2000; Tue–Sat 0900–0200; Sun 0900–2400. ££.

Spain gets the theme-park treatment at this fake 'Spanish Village', designed as the arts and crafts section of the 1929 International Exhibition. Critics complain that it glorifies Spanish rather than Catalan culture, but it is important to remember that it was conceived by **Josep Puig i Cadafalch**, a Catalan nationalist who was the original architect of the exhibition, as a way of emphasising the diversity of the Spanish nation and celebrating its different cultures. It is undeniably touristy, and in summer it is packed out with tour groups from the Costa Brava beaches, but it is no less enjoyable for that – and though a stroll around the Barri Gòtic would be considerably more authentic, it also serves as a useful introduction to the various styles of Spanish architecture.

The basic idea was to include **vernacular architecture** and **copies of historic buildings** from the various Spanish regions, grouped together in streets with a distinctive regional flavour. You enter through a Romanesque gateway from Avila and a Gothic portico from Navarra to reach a main square from Segovia lined with Renaissance palaces and an Aragonese town hall. As you wander around the village, you come across solid Basque farmhouses, whitewashed Andalusian patios, a Mudéjar (Moorish–Gothic) bell-tower from Zaragoza and a famous fountain from Tarragona. There is even a Catalan Romanesque monastery, complete with cloister.

Scattered throughout the 'village' are craft workshops and souvenir shops selling typical Spanish products such as ceramics, glassware and lace, along with more tourist-oriented items like football shirts, flamenco costumes and castanets. It is easy to dismiss all of this as tourist kitsch, but as some commentators have pointed out, it is actually quite authentic. After all, the very streets in Seville and Madrid on which these imitations are modelled are probably full of souvenir shops themselves by now.

There is a good choice of eating places chosen to fit in with the themes, featuring Cuban cooking, Andalusian *tapas* and traditional Catalan cuisine as well as sandwiches and bar snacks. In the evenings there is also a cabaret show, and a flamenco spectacular, **El Tablao de Carmen**, for which it is advisable to book (*tel: 93 325 6895; closed Mon; £££*).

> " *An uninterrupted barrage of the clichés of PoMo irony – as though Philippe Starck at his most morbid teamed up with Peter Eisenmann at his most hostile to do the sets for Pee-wee's Playhouse.* "
>
> **Robert Hughes on Torres de Avila, *Barcelona*, 1992**

By the 1980s the Poble Espanyol was starting to look rather shabby, so it was given a facelift by the city's pre-Olympic architects and reinvented as a lively nightlife quarter. The most dramatic example of this is **Torres de Avila**, a nightclub and disco situated inside the 'medieval' gateway. Designed by **Xavier Mariscal** and opened in 1990, this is Barcelona's ultimate designer bar, with moving walls, hanging steel staircases and transparent glass in the toilets. It has been described by Barcelona historian Robert Hughes as 'the most seriously unenjoyable *boîte de nuit* in Spain, or maybe the world', but it remains one of the hottest spots in town on a Friday or Saturday night. Just remember, if you do go to the Gents', do up your flies before turning round.

Plaça d'Espanya

The present-day layout of Montjuïc has its origins in the International Exhibition of 1929, and the best place to begin a tour is at this huge square, designed by Josep Puig i Cadafalch as a grand entrance to the exhibition. The dominant architectural theme of the time was noucentisme, *a reaction against Modernism and a return to classical styles, and this is reflected in the square.*

The monumental fountain at the centre was designed by Josep Maria Jujol, a colleague of Gaudí's, with marble and bronze sculptures by Miquel Blay representing Spain's great rivers. By contrast, the nearby Les Arenes bullring, now fallen into disuse, was built in 1900 in neo-Moorish style. The twin towers at the entrance to Avinguda Reina Maria Cristina were modelled on Venetian campaniles and act as the gateway to the exhibition buildings. The pavilions to either side, built in 1929, remain in use as trade fairs today.

The avenue leads to Plaça Carles Buïgas, named after the engineer responsible for the Font Màgica ('Magic Fountain'), one of the best-loved features of the 1929 Exhibition. The illuminated fountain is still the centrepiece of a spectacular sound-and-light show, which takes place on summer evenings and at weekends throughout the year, when the water appears to dance to the music of Holst and Tchaikovsky. The performance is free, but extremely popular. Arrive early for a good view.

On the right of the fountain as you look up towards Montjuïc, the **Pavelló Mies van der Rohe** (*open: Apr–Oct, 1000–2000 daily; Sept–Mar, 1000–1800 daily; £*) was designed by Ludwig Mies van der Rohe as the German pavilion and is considered a classic example of the rationalist style. With its simple, low-slung design in stone, marble and glass, it stands in stark contrast to the neo-classical pomposity of the surrounding buildings. The pavilion you see is actually a replica dating from 1986; the original was dismantled after the 1929 Exhibition.

Above the fountain, a series of terraced waterfalls cascades down from Montjuïc and an escalator carries you up to the Palau Nacional for views over the square. On the way you pass the twin pavilions of **Queen Victoria Eugenia** and **King Alfonso XIII**, designed, like so much around here, by Puig i Cadafalch.

Tip

As well as being an architect, Josep Puig i Cadafalch was also a politician. From 1917 to 1924 he was president of the Mancomunitat, a Catalan administrative government dissolved by the dictator Primo de la Rivera shortly after he came to power in 1923.

L'EIXAMPLE

L'Eixample

The Eixample ('extension') was devised in the 19th century, when Barcelona expanded beyond the limits of the medieval walls. It was here that the Modernist architects were given free rein to develop their fantasies.

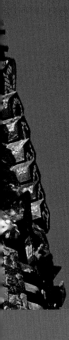

BEST OF

L'Eixample

Getting there: most of the main attractions are spread out along Passeig de Gràcia, so it is best to take the Metro to Catalunya, Diagonal or Passeig de Gràcia and then walk along this street. The two exceptions, Sagrada Família and Hospital de Sant Pau, are situated some distance away in the old Poblet district. Each of them has its own Metro station, reached by line 5 from Diagonal, and they are also connected by an attractive promenade. Although it is possible to walk from Passeig de Gràcia to the Sagrada Família, the rigid street plan and the number of roads you have to cross make it more tiring than you would expect.

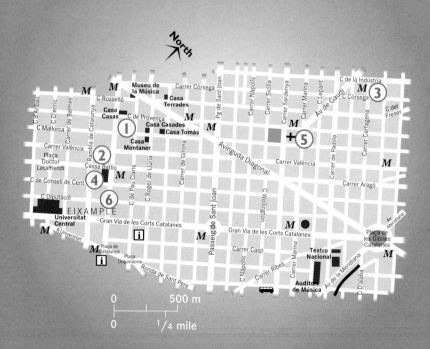

1 Casa Milà

This Gaudí-designed apartment building makes an excellent introduction to Modernist architecture, and also contains an exhibition relating to Gaudí's life and work. The rooftop terrace, with its ceramic chimneys, is typical of Gaudí's style. **Pages 120–1**

2 Fundació Antoni Tàpies

Although Gaudí grabs most of the headlines, many people consider his contemporary **Lluís Domènech i Montaner** to be the truest exponent of the Modernist art. His first building in Barcelona is now a museum devoted to Catalonia's best-known abstract artist. **Page 122**

3 Hospital de Sant Pau

The largest Modernist complex in Barcelona is a working hospital, more like a miniature city with pavilions set around peaceful gardens. Doctors and patients stroll around the grounds, almost oblivious to the magnificent architecture around them. **Page 123**

4 Mançana de la Discòrdia

The holy trinity of Modernist architects has produced a mêlée of clashing styles in a single block of houses along Passeig de Gràcia. This is the starting point of the **Ruta del Modernisme**, a complete tour of Barcelona's Modernist buildings. **Pages 124–5, 130–1**

5 Sagrada Família

What more can you say about this remarkable unfinished cathedral, the culmination of Gaudí's creative genius? Long after his death, it continues to arouse controversy, as the architects and builders work on in an attempt to realise Gaudí's dream. **Pages 126–7**

6 Passeig de Gràcia shopping

A stroll along Passeig de Gràcia is not only an opportunity to see Modernist architecture but also to shop in Barcelona's most elegant boutiques. This boulevard has long been the city's swankiest shopping street, lined with stores selling the latest fashions and designs. **Page 129**

Tip

If you are interested in Modernist architecture, make sure to buy a ticket for the Ruta del Modernisme (see pages 130–1). As well as guided tours and discounted entry to attractions, the ticket includes an English-language guidebook to some 50 Modernist buildings.

Casa Milà

Passeig de Gràcia 92. Tel: 93 484 5995. Metro: Diagonal. Open: 1000–2000 daily. £££.

This apartment block designed by **Antoni Gaudí** is as good a place as any to begin a tour of the Modernist quarter and develop an understanding of Gaudi's unique style. Built between 1906 and 1912 for the businessman Pere Milà, this was Gaudi's last major secular work and possibly his greatest. Derided at the time and nicknamed **La Pedrera** ('the stone quarry') because of its wavy architecture and lack of straight lines, the building's reputation has grown over the years and it is now considered a masterpiece, its **undulating stone façade** and **twisted wrought-iron balconies** one of the most emblematic sights of Barcelona.

The building has been thoroughly restored in recent years by the Fundació Caixa Catalunya, a cultural foundation established and funded by a leading Catalan bank. A full visit begins with a tour of two sixth-floor apartments. The first houses an exhibition placing Modernism in its context at a time of rapid economic and technological change (telephones, electricity, the Metro, department stores); the second, which is surprisingly spacious, attempts to recreate the furnishing of a typical upper-class flat in the early 20th century. From here you climb to the loft, designed as a laundry but more like a Gothic cathedral with its soaring parabolic brick arches. This part of the building is now the

Espai Gaudí, an exhibition of Gaudí's life and work. Of particular interest are the photographs showing the interiors of buildings that are normally closed to the public, including the nearby **Casa Batlló** (*see page 125*).

The high point of the visit, in more ways than one, is the **rooftop terrace**, with its chimneys and ventilation shafts fashioned out of ceramic fragments, Cava bottles and pieces of broken marble. There are chimneys in the shape of owls, and a central chimney based on the cross of St George, Catalonia's patron saint. Gaudí had wanted to give the building more of a religious focus, with a sculptured figure of the Virgin on the roof, but Milà refused owing to the anarchist fervour of the time. From the terrace there are good views of Barcelona, including Gaudí's other great masterpiece, the nearby **Sagrada Família** (*see pages 126–7*). Between July and September, the terrace is also open in the evenings (*Fri–Sat 2100–0000*), a popular place for a pre-dinner drink with live music and a rooftop bar.

Afterwards, be sure to visit **Casa Casas** (*Passeig de Gràcia 96*), built in 1899 by Antoni Rovira for the Modernist painter Ramon Casas. This is now the home of **Vinçon**, Barcelona's leading design store, known for its cutting-edge designs in furniture and household goods. An art gallery, **Sala Vinçon** (*open: Tue–Sat 1000–1400, 1630–2030, closed Mon*), in Casas' original studio, hosts regular exhibitions of avant-garde furniture and design; it was here that **Xavier Mariscal**, designer of the Olympic mascot and many of Barcelona's best-known designer bars, made his name as a student in the 1970s. If you wander up to the first-floor furniture department and step out on to the interior patio, there is a great view of Casa Milà from a different angle. There's no need to be embarrassed; everyone does it.

121

Fundació Antoni Tàpies

Carrer d'Aragó 255. Tel: 93 487 0315. Metro: Passeig de Gràcia. Open: Tue–Sun 1000–2000; closed Mon. ££.

The first major work in Barcelona by **Lluís Domènech i Montaner** is widely seen as initiating the Modernist architectural movement. It was built between 1880 and 1885 using **ironwork clad in brick**, a revolutionary design that had previously been seen only in railway stations and market halls. The Modernist touches stemmed not just from the industrial materials, but also the Mudéjar (Moorish–Gothic) influence in the brickwork and the rose windows designed to resemble cog-wheels. Inside, the spacious floors are supported by factory-style columns, and a pyramid skylight lets in the sun.

The building now houses an art gallery established by Antoni Tàpies, who was born in Barcelona in 1923 and went on to become one of Spain's leading abstract artists. An enormous twisted wire sculpture by Tàpies, *Núvol i Cadira* ('Cloud

and Chair'), adorns the roof; inside there are more of his works on display, mostly large-scale collages based on plain black or white backgrounds but with the addition of everyday objects hanging from the canvas. Only a small part of the Tàpies collection is on display at any one time, as the gallery also hosts regular exhibitions of cutting-edge contemporary art. The foundation is also devoted to the study of non-Western art forms, and the upstairs library is always full of students, poring over its large collection of texts on oriental arts and mysticism.

Hospital de Sant Pau

Carrer de Sant Antoni Maria Claret 167. Tel: 93 291 9000. Metro: Hospital de Sant Pau. Admission free.

The largest Modernist complex in Barcelona was also designed by Domènech i Montaner, though it was eventually completed by his son Pere Domènech after his death. Along with the Palau de la Música Catalana (*see pages 72–3*), this was the project which established Montaner as a Modernist genius on a par with Gaudi.

The money was provided by the Catalan banker Pau Gil, who left funds for a new hospital to ease the pressure on the Hospital de la Santa Creu in El Raval (*see page 40*). The idea was to create a garden city, with separate pavilions for the various hospital departments, set in the midst of peaceful gardens and linked by a series of underground tunnels. The entire complex was designed in a mock-Byzantine style, with brick vaulting and typically Modernist ceramic domes and roofs.

> " *Here, in balmy weather, patients in pyjamas wander with their visitors under the shady trees, passing, to take one example, the vascular surgery department, decked out harmoniously but surprisingly with spires and cupolas.* "

Adam Hopkins, *Spanish Journeys*, 1992

The fascination of wandering around this place is that it is still very much a working hospital; one minute you are looking at the architecture, the next at doctors in white coats, signs for the blood bank and patients in dressing gowns who have slipped out for a cigarette. Naturally, much of the hospital is out of bounds to casual visitors, but the gardens are always open and make a pleasant spot. You can also go into the main vestibule, where a grand staircase leads to an upper hallway; look out of the windows along a promenade, Avinguda de Gaudi, which leads to the Sagrada Família (*see pages 126–7*). It is interesting to note that both the promenade and the hospital are set diagonally against the surrounding streets, posing a deliberate challenge to the strict 19th-century grid plan of the Eixample.

Mançana de la Discòrdia

Passeig de Gràcia 35–43. Metro: Passeig de Gràcia.

The rivalry between the three leading Modernist architects at the turn of the 20th century produced a remarkable ensemble of buildings which come together on a single block known as 'Mançana de la Discòrdia'. The name is a clever pun on the double meaning of the word *mançana* (*manzana* in Spanish). Its usual meaning is 'apple', and 'apple of discord' is the Spanish phrase equivalent to 'bone of contention' in English. At the same time, the word can also mean 'a block of houses' – and the discord refers to the clashing styles of these three very different architects.

Although you can see only the external façades of the three buildings, it is still worth visiting them on a guided tour at the start of the Ruta del Modernisme (*see pages 130–1*) in order to appreciate the symbolism involved. Start with **Casa Lleó Morera** (*No 35; not open to the public*), designed by **Domènech i Montaner** in 1902 for the Lleó Morera family. Lions and mulberry trees on the façade are a reference to the family name, while sculpted figures of women holding a light bulb and a camera are symbols of technological progress. The first-floor rooms, designed as the family's private apartments, are usually closed to visitors, but they are a glorious example of Modernist art, richly adorned with mosaics, ceramics and stained glass. The ground-floor façade, with sculptures by Eusebi Arnau, was destroyed by the Loewe leather goods company when it opened its shop here in 1943, an act of cultural vandalism for which it has never been forgiven.

The second house, Casa Amatller (*No 41; see page 130*), was designed by Josep Puig i Cadafalch in 1898 for the chocolate manufacturer Antoni Amatller. The façade is a strange mix of neo-Gothic and Dutch gabled styles, with patriotic symbols including the rose and the legend of St George. The vestibule is open during the day as the offices of the Ruta del Modernisme; go inside to admire the Modernist skylight and the second oldest working lift in Barcelona. Also in the hallway are gargoyles depicting characters making chocolate, eating chocolate and being sick – a joke at the expense of Senyor Amatller.

Finally you come to Casa Batlló (*No 43; not open to the public*), designed by Gaudi in 1905 and featuring all his familiar trademarks, from broken ceramics to undulating waves. Gaudi's fantasies run riot here, from a rooftop shaped like a dragon to balconies in the shape of carnival masks. If you really want a special location for a party, you can rent out the first-floor rooms.

Museu de la Música

Avinguda Diagonal 373. Tel: 93 416 1157. Metro: Diagonal. Open: Tue–Sun 1000–1400; Wed 1400–2000 Oct–June only. £.

This museum, housed in Puig i Cadafalch's neo-Gothic Palau del Baró de Quadras, has a collection of some 1 500 musical instruments. The highlight is the collection of guitars, one of the finest in the world, dating back to the origins of the instrument in 17th-century Spain. Also on display are the various wind instruments used in the *coble*, the 11-piece orchestra that accompanies the Catalan *sardana* dance. There are also Galician bagpipes, Andalusian castanets, Cuban maracas, African drums and a fine collection of baroque Spanish organs, displayed in a sumptuous Modernist drawing-room overlooking the street.

Sagrada Família

Carrer de Mallorca 401. Tel: 93 207 3031. Metro: Sagrada Família. Open:
Nov–Feb, 0900–1800 daily; Mar, Sept–Oct, 0900–1900 daily; Apr–Aug,
0900–2000 daily. ££.

A building site, a Modernist triumph or a monumental folly
and overblown tourist trap which would not be nearly so
interesting if it had been finished? Long after his death,
Gaudi's unfinished masterpiece continues to arouse strong
feelings. For George Orwell, it was 'one of the most hideous
buildings in the world'; for many visitors to Barcelona, it
is the highlight of their visit and the symbol of all that the
city represents.

What comes as a surprise to many is that Antoni Gaudi,
the playful designer of Park Güell (*see pages 138–9*), was a
deeply religious man. Appointed in 1883 as chief architect of
the cathedral, he devoted the last 40 years of his life to it and
from 1914 refused to take on any other work, giving up his
salary and living in a worker's hut on the site, driven on by
spiritual fervour. When asked why the cathedral was taking
so long, he replied: 'My client is in no hurry'. When asked why
he lavished so much attention on the mosaic spires that
nobody could see: 'The angels will see them'. It is fitting that
he was on his way to Vespers when he was run down by a
tram in 1926; he died three days later and is buried beneath
the nave. In recent years, Catalan bishops have begun the
first steps that could lead to Gaudi being declared a saint.

Gaudí's plans were incredibly ambitious, with 18 crenellated towers and an enormous central nave. Only the crypt, apse and part of the Nativity façade were completed during Gaudí's lifetime. The Nativity façade, with exquisite stone carvings full of religious symbolism yet with the appearance of a fairy grotto, is the undoubted high point of the building. Incidentally, if you want to see just the façades, there is no need to pay the entrance fee, as the views are better from outside.

Many of Gaudí's plans for the cathedral were destroyed during the Civil War – though the church miraculously survived – making the work which resumed in the 1950s all the more controversial. Should it be left alone as a testament to Gaudí's genius, or should it be completed by a later generation? The Passion façade, with sculptures by Josep Subirachs, was finished in 1990 and has been the focus of considerable comment. Many people accuse Subirachs' modern sculptures of being tasteless and out of keeping with their environment, but then that was exactly what people said about Gaudí.

In any case, the work is being completed and the inside of the cathedral resembles a building site. You can climb the towers or take the lift to a viewing platform for a close-up look at the spires, then peer down into the nave to see the work in progress. The plan is to cover the nave and transepts by the end of 2000; the entire building should be roofed by 2010. The architect Jordi Bonet is working on a new Glory façade. Eventually, a great dome will support a 160m (525ft) tower, surpassing the Olympic skyscrapers and making this once again the tallest building in Barcelona. Now what would Gaudí say to that?

127

Restaurants

Asador de Burgos
Carrer del Bruc 118. Tel: 93 207 3160.
£££. Vegetarians should steer well clear of this Castilian-style roast house, while serious carnivores will love it. The specialities include *cocido castellano* (a stew with bacon, *chorizo* and blood sausage) and roast lamb slow-cooked in a traditional wood oven.

Bistrot 106
Carrer d'Aribau 106. Tel: 93 453 2323. ££. Everything is *très Parisien* at this intimate French bistro, with modern art on the walls, Piaf on the gramophone and a menu featuring snails *bourguignonne*, beef *charolaise* and *crêpes suzettes* for dessert.

Casa Calvet
Carrer de Casp 48. Tel: 93 412 4012.
£££. Gaudí's first apartment building in the Eixample is now a formal restaurant, offering creative modern Catalan cuisine in authentic Modernist splendour. Among the specialities are partridge with chestnuts and oyster ravioli in Cava.

Centro Asturiano de Barcelona
Passeig de Gràcia 78. Tel: 93 215 3010. ££. For honest, down-to-earth cooking, try this Asturian cultural centre with a terrace overlooking the street. The lunch menu features northern Spanish classics such as bean stew and grilled steaks, accompanied by a glass of strong Asturian cider.

Kowloon
Carrer d'Aribau 115. Tel: 93 453 1753.
££. One of the top Chinese restaurants in Spain, this was used as the official base of the Chinese delegation during the 1992 Olympics. It features creative versions of Chinese cuisine, such as steamed lobster in oyster sauce and sea-bass with black-bean sauce.

Tragaluz
Passatge de la Concepció 5. Tel: 93 487 0621. ££. This deeply hip restaurant offers eclectic Catalan–Japanese cuisine in a Renaissance palace given a new look by design star Xavier Mariscal. The bar serves 'Japanese *tapas*' and the restaurant features unusual dishes such as sole in red wine sauce. The same owners have a more authentically Japanese place, **El Japonès**, across the street.

Designer bars

The concept of the 'designer bar' had its origins in style-conscious Barcelona during the 1980s. At one time, a crawl around the designer bars of L'Eixample was the hottest night out in town, and though the bars are now considered deeply passé, *they have developed a certain retro appeal (* see page 177 *).*

Tapas bars

The lower end of Passeig de Gràcia has several *tapas* bars, with tables out on the street to catch the afternoon sun. One of the best is Tapa Tapa (*Passeig de Gràcia 44*), with a large range of hot and cold snacks such as shrimp croquettes, garlic mushrooms and chicken in whisky. Ba-ba-reeba (*Passeig de Gràcia 28*) serves *tapas* and grills such as salmon or steak and chips, while Quasi Queviures (*Passeig de Gràcia 24*), commonly known as QuQu, is a delicatessen, *tapas* bar and restaurant rolled into one. Txapela (*Passeig de Gràcia 8–10*) has latched on to the Basque *tapas* craze sweeping Barcelona and offers a menu of more than 50 *pintxos*, but you have to choose from a picture menu rather than help yourself from the bar. Two older and more authentic places in the back streets of L'Eixample are Café del Centre (*Carrer de Girona 69*), an old gambling hall where the speciality is a wooden board of cold cuts with toasted bread, and Casa Alfonso (*Carrer Roger de Llúria 6*), a classic local bar with hams hanging from the ceiling and a simple menu of sandwiches and charcoal grills.

Shopping

Many of the top boutiques in Barcelona are found along the parallel promenades of Passeig de Gràcia and Rambla de Catalunya. On Passeig de Gràcia, look out for Adolfo Domínguez (*No 32*), one of the top names in Spanish fashion for men and women; Loewe (*No 35*), in the ground floor of Casa Lleó Morera, for leather bags, jackets and shoes; and Bagués (*No 41*), a Modernist jewellers' shop in the ground floor of Casa Amatller. Not far from here, the Centre Català d'Artesania (*No 55*) is a large, bright gallery highlighting the best in contemporary Catalan design, including jewellery, ceramics and glassware. Barcelona's design temple, Vinçon (*No 96; see page 121*) is further up the street.

Colmado Quilez (*Rambla de Catalunya 63*) is Barcelona's most famous grocery store, with a phenomenal range of cold meats, cheeses and wines, and tinned goods stacked from floor to ceiling. Another wonderful food shop is Queviures Murrià (*Carrer Roger de Llúria 86*), a Modernist landmark with a shopfront by Ramon Casas and separate counters selling cheese, wine and coffee. And wine-lovers should not miss Xampany (*Carrer de València 200*), more like a museum of Cava than a shop, with cabinets full of champagne bottles, labels and corks.

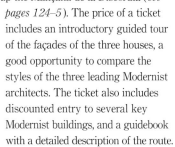

PROFILE

La Ruta del Modernisme

Modernism was a surprisingly democratic style of architecture, seen in markets, wine cellars and pastry-shops as well as apartment blocks, upper-class mansions and hotels. There are more than a thousand Modernist buildings scattered around Barcelona, most of them in the Eixample, but most visitors only get to see a few. To remedy this situation, the authorities have devised a tourist route that covers all the main sights of Modernism and a good sprinkling of lesser ones too.

The Modernist Route begins in **Casa Amatller** (*Passeig de Gràcia 41; tel: 93 488 0139; open: Mon–Sat 1000–1900, Sun 1000–1400; tours on the hour; ££*), one of the three houses which make up the Mançana de la Discòrdia (*see pages 124–5*). The price of a ticket includes an introductory guided tour of the façades of the three houses, a good opportunity to compare the styles of the three leading Modernist architects. The ticket also includes discounted entry to several key Modernist buildings, and a guidebook with a detailed description of the route.

There are various suggested diversions along the way, but the main route involves a walk of some 3.5km (2 ½ miles) followed by Metro and bus journeys to the outlying sights. The entire route can just about be done in a day, but the ticket is valid for a month, allowing you to tackle it in several small stages.

L'EIXAMPLE

The route takes you into the furthest reaches of the Eixample, where there are more buildings by the 'big three' Modernist architects. **Casa Vicens** (*Carrer de les Carolines 24; Metro: Fontana*) in Gràcia was one of Gaudí's earliest commissions, built between 1883 and 1888 for the industrialist Manuel Vicens, and full of Islamic-style designs in ceramics and brick. **Casa Fuster** (*Passeig de Gràcia 132; Metro: Diagonal*), by Domènech i Montaner, is a neo-Gothic house with a Venetian white-marble façade. **Casa Terrades** (*Avinguda Diagonal 416; Metro: Diagonal*) is Puig i Cadafalch's best-known work in Barcelona, nicknamed Casa de les Punxes ('House of the Spikes') because of the turrets and spires which give it the appearance of a medieval castle.

" *Barcelona has been called to be the Athens of Modernism.* "

From *L'Esquella de la Torratxa* magazine, 1909

Greater Barcelona

The outskirts of Barcelona contain several interesting sights, including a medieval monastery, a mountain overlooking the city, and the home of Barcelona's celebrated football team.

133

Greater Barcelona

Getting there: the sights in this chapter are fairly spread out, and not all of them are easily reached by public transport, so taxis may be a better option. The main sights are all featured on the northern (red) route of the Bus Turístic, which links up with the tram to Tibidabo.

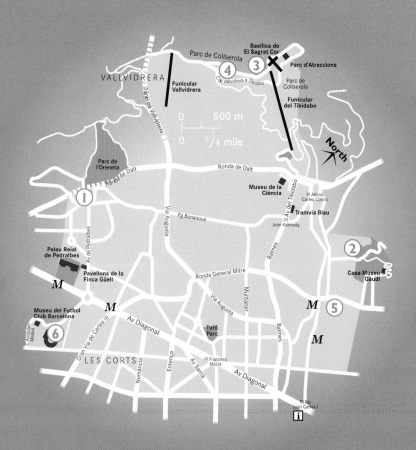

① Monestir de Pedralbes

The last surviving monastic complex in Barcelona is still home to a community of nuns, as well as a superb collection of medieval art. A chapel off the cloister contains 14th-century frescos by the Catalan painter Ferrer Bassa. **Page 136**

② Park Güell

Nowhere is Gaudí's sense of playfulness more in evidence than in this fantastical country park, designed as a garden city with dragon stairways, twisting mosaic benches and fairy-tale pavilions. The house where Gaudí lived is now a museum devoted to his work. **Pages 138-9**

③ Tibidabo

When the people of Barcelona want to escape the city, they head for this mountain, with its funfair, fresh air and panoramic views. The ascent of Tibidabo, on a rickety old tram and a funicular mountain railway, is half the fun of the trip. **Pages 140-1**

④ Torre de Collserola

Norman Foster's elegant communications tower is visible from across the city, its giant needle pointing upwards to the sky. On a clear day, the views from the observation gallery stretch from the mountain of Montserrat to the island of Mallorca. **Page 141**

⑤ Gràcia

This former working-class village has long been associated with radical politics, providing a breeding-ground for anarchists and revolutionaries in the 19th century. These days it is a bohemian suburb of writers and artists, a good place for a lively night out among the wholefood *tapas* bars and ethnic restaurants. **Pages 142-3**

⑥ Camp Nou

FC Barcelona is more than a football club, and Camp Nou is more than a stadium – it is the cathedral of Catalan soccer. The club museum tells the story of the great players and personalities of the past, and the symbolic role that 'Barça' continues to play in Catalan society. **Pages 144-5**

Tip

It is best to treat these attractions as a series of day trips from the city, and not try to do too much in one go. If you want to see them all in a day, however, buy a ticket for the Bus Turístic and follow the northern (red) route, which leads anticlockwise past Park Güell and Tibidabo to Pedralbes and Camp Nou, and returns along Avinguda Diagonal towards Gràcia. This is good as a scenic route, but although you can hop on and off as many times as you like, you are unlikely to have enough time to explore all the sights.

Monestir de Pedralbes

Baixada del Monestir 9. Tel: 93 280 1434. FGC: Reina Elisenda. Bus: 22, 63, 64, 75. Open: Tue–Sun 1000–1400; closed Mon. £.

Barcelona's only surviving medieval monastery was founded in 1326 by Queen Elisenda, the fourth and last wife of Jaume II of Aragón. The queen herself is buried in the church, her lavish tomb decorated with reliefs depicting the dead monarch being mourned by angels. The various chapels and monastery buildings are grouped around a three-storey Gothic cloister, completed in the 15th century.

The highlight is the Capella de Sant Miquel, a tiny chapel decorated with frescos by the court painter Ferrer Bassa, creator of the Italian-Gothic style in Catalonia. The remarkably well-preserved frescos, featuring scenes from Christ's Passion and the life of the Virgin, were completed in 1346, two years before Bassa's death from the plague. You can also visit the 15th-century refectory – where as recently as 1983 the nuns would eat in silence while one of their number read from the pulpit – and a 16th-century Renaissance infirmary.

Since 1993 the monastery has housed the Collecció Thyssen-Bornemisza (*open same hours as monastery; £*), a collection of mostly religious art from the medieval to baroque periods. The collection, housed in the nuns' old dormitory, is small and manageable but contains several

You can walk from the monastery to the palace along Avinguda de Pedralbes, a wide avenue at the heart of an exclusive residential quarter. Along the way you pass the entrance to Finca Güell, Count Güell's country estate, with a pair of Modernist pavilions by Gaudí and an extraordinary wrought-iron dragon on the gates.

minor masterpieces, making it very appealing to visit. The strength of the collection is European old masters, including Fra Angelico, Cranach, Titian, Tintoretto, Rubens, Velázquez and Canaletto. The oldest pieces on display are an anonymous 13th-century sculpture of the Virgin and Child from northern France, and a 13th-century Umbrian polychrome figure of the dead Christ.

Palau Reial de Pedralbes

Avinguda Diagonal 686. Metro: Palau Reial.

This extravagant Italianate mansion was built for Gaudi's patron Count Eusebi Güell, who later donated it to Alfonso XIII for use as the royal family's summer palace. After the Civil War it became Franco's official residence in Barcelona, and it briefly returned to royal use in 1997 when it hosted the wedding banquet of the *infanta* Princess Cristina.

The gardens (*open: 1000–2000 daily in summer, 1000–1800 in winter; admission free*), with their sculptures, ponds and shady walkways, make a tranquil and pleasant retreat, popular with courting couples and students from the nearby university who come here to read their books beneath the eucalyptus trees. In a quiet corner of the gardens there is a fountain by Antoni Gaudí, designed around 1884 and discovered almost a hundred years later hidden in the undergrowth.

The palace now contains a pair of specialist museums, which can be visited on a combined ticket. The Museu de Ceràmica (*tel: 93 280 1621; open: Tue–Sat 1000–1800, Sun 1000–1500, closed Mon; £*) features a collection of Spanish pottery from the 11th century to the present day, including pieces by Miró and Picasso, while the Museu de les Arts Decoratives (*tel: 93 280 5024; same hours; £*) is devoted to furniture and domestic arts, from medieval times to modern industrial design.

Park Güell

Carrer d'Olot. Metro: Vallcarca. Bus: 24, 25. Open: 1000 to dusk, daily.
Admission free.

Of all Antoni Gaudí's contributions to Barcelona, none is more enjoyable than this park overlooking the city. It was commissioned in 1900 by his patron Count Eusebi Güell, whose idea was to create a fashionable residential district along the lines of English garden cities – hence the use of 'park' instead of its Spanish or Catalan equivalents. In the event, the project was a failure, and only two of the sixty houses were completed before Güell's death in 1918. Four years later, the entire plot was taken over by the city of Barcelona and turned into a municipal park.

It was here that Gaudí's sense of playfulness was given full rein, in a riot of Disneyesque fantasy. The main entrance on Carrer d'Olot is flanked by a **pair of gatehouses** based on Gaudí's drawings for the fairy-tale 'Hansel and Gretel'. On the left is the children's house, with a double cross on the roof; on the right, the house of the witch, topped by a fly agaric mushroom, which Eusebi Güell liked to collect. It is tempting to suggest that Gaudí must have been well acquainted with these mushrooms, which are known for their hallucinogenic qualities.

Inside the gates, a double stairway divided by a waterfall is watched over by a colourful **mosaic dragon**, the symbol of the park. Children love climbing on the dragon, and tourists pose for pictures on the steps. The stairway leads to the **Hall of Columns**, a cool space designed as a market hall but more like a Greek temple, with inlaid patterns of broken glass and mosaics on the ceiling. Above this is the park's high point, the **central esplanade** surrounded by an

undulating bench, created by Gaudí and his assistant Josep Maria Jujol out of his trademark *trencadis* – pieces of broken ceramic rearranged to form abstract patterns and shapes. Around the square, a labyrinth of shady passages is enclosed by avenues of columns, leaning into the hillside to give the impression of a series of natural caves.

The artist **Salvador Dalí** loved to stroll here while looking for inspiration for his paintings. Although most people tend to gather around the main square, you can easily lose yourself for hours, discovering secret paths and gazing down at Barcelona through the trees.

> *His brain is at the tips of his fingers and tongue.* ,,
> **Salvador Dalí (1904–89) on Antoni Gaudí**

Afterwards, visit **Casa-Museu Gaudí** (*open: Oct–May, 1000–1800 daily; June–Sept, 1000–2000; £*), the house where Gaudí lived for the last 20 years of his life, though he actually spent most of his time in a hut at the Sagrada Família. On a tour of the house, you can see Gaudí's bedroom, study and death-mask, as well as examples of furniture he designed.

There are two ways of getting to the park by public transport. The **bus** (*No 24 from Plaça de Catalunya*) drops you off outside the side entrance on Carretera de Carmel, a good place to begin a tour of the park before ending up at the main sights. Alternatively, take the **Metro** to Vallcarca, walk down Avinguda de l'Hospital Militar, and follow the signs up Baixada de la Glòria – a steep climb, but outdoor escalators will take you some of the way. At the top of the hill, climb the steps opposite to enter the park and follow the path on your right for views over the esplanade before reaching the main entrance on Carrer d'Olot.

Tibidabo

FGC to Avinguda del Tibidabo, followed by tram and funicular.

The mountain at the summit of the Serra de Collserola range has been a playground for the people of Barcelona for more than a hundred years. It all began in 1901, when the pill manufacturer Dr Andreu invested some of his fortune in developing the tramway and the funicular railway that brought Tibidabo within day-trip distance of the city. Soon afterwards, Spain's first funfair appeared on the peak, and people began to head there at weekends for old-fashioned entertainment and great views.

Getting to Tibidabo is half the fun of this trip. From the train station, cross Plaça John Kennedy, notable for the Modernist

façade and mosaic dome of the Sant Gervasi hospital, better known as **La Rotonda**. This brings you out by the stop for the **Tramvia Blau**, Barcelona's last surviving tram and a charming relic of the early 20th century. Except in summer, the tram service only operates at weekends; buses are laid on during the week instead. The tram trundles up Avinguda del Tibidabo, passing the Modernist mansions of Barcelona's wealthy, many of them converted into restaurants, offices and foreign consulates.

You can ask to be let off close to the **Museu de la Ciència** (*Carrer Teodor Roviralta 55; open: Tue–Sun 1000–2000, closed Mon; ££*), an interactive science museum with hands-on exhibits, a planetarium and a scientific playground for younger kids.

The tram stops in **Plaça Dr Andreu**, a square lined with café terraces overlooking the city. From here you can take a funicular to the summit. The funicular operates whenever the funfair is open and also on winter weekends. It ends close to the **Parc d'Atraccions** (*open: Easter to Oct, Sat–Sun 1200–2000; extended hours throughout summer period; July–Aug, 1200–0100 daily; £££*), still as popular as ever with its ferris wheel, haunted castle and ancient fairground rides. A ride

Tip

Tibidabo takes its name from the words said to have been spoken by the Devil to Christ when he tried to tempt him with the world at his feet:
haec omnia tibi dabo si cadens adoraberis me
('all this will I give you, if you fall down and worship me').

on the 'aeroplane', with the city spread out beneath you, is a memorable if scary experience, especially when you remember that it has been operating since 1928.

Behind the park, the **basilica of El Sagrat Cor** ('Sacred Heart') is a part-Gothic, part-Modernist church, topped by a giant statue of Christ which seems to have been built more for the glory of Spain than the glory of God. You can climb the steps behind the basilica for magnificent views.

Torre de Collserola

Carretera de Vallvidrera a Tibidabo. Tel: 93 406 9354. Bus: 211 from Tibidabo or Vallvidrera. Open: Wed–Sun 1100–1800. ££.

To complete a day out on Tibidabo, walk or take the bus down to this elegant communications tower, designed by the British architect **Norman Foster** for the 1992 Olympics and known by the locals as 'Torre Foster'. Little more than a steel mast built into a concrete block, it stands 288m (945ft) high on its own small summit. A lift whisks you up to the observatory, 560m (1 835ft) above sea level, where the 360-degree views stretch from Montserrat to Mallorca – though all too often even Barcelona is obscured by a pollution-induced haze.

From here there are various waymarked walks on the Collserola massif, in the **Parc de Collserola**, whose information centre is close to the nearby hilltop town of Vallvidrera. To return to Barcelona by a different route, continue to Vallvidrera by bus or on foot and take the old wooden funicular, dating from 1906, to rejoin the FGC railway network at Peu del Funicular.

Restaurants

The former township of Gràcia *has long had a reputation for radicalism, and a streak of individuality that reveals itself in the variety of its restaurants. Some of the top establishments in the city are situated here, along with a number of offbeat choices that appeal to the local population of students, artists and intellectuals. The best Metro station for Gràcia is Fontana.*

Botafumeiro
Carrer Gran de Gràcia 81. Tel: 93 218 4230. £££. This famous Galician seafood restaurant is housed inside one of several Modernist mansions along Gràcia's main street. The menu features caviar, lobster and black paella, as well as exquisite sea-bass and sea-bream cooked on an open grill. Booking is essential.

Jean Luc Figueras
Carrer Santa Teresa 10. Tel: 93 415 2877. £££. This gastronomic temple is situated inside a neo-classical palace, contributing to an atmosphere of refined elegance. The French chef Jean Luc Figueras turns out perfect French–Catalan cuisine, with signature dishes including lobster pancake and an unexpected blend of sea-bass, salt-cod tripe and Catalan blood sausage.

La Buena Tierra
Carrer de l'Encarnació 56. Tel: 93 219 8213. £. This intimate vegetarian restaurant (its name means 'the good earth') is more like a private house, with a cosy little dining-room and a pretty summer garden. The four-course lunch menu is particularly good value.

L'Illa de Gràcia
Carrer Sant Domenec 19. Tel: 93 238 0229. £. This funky vegetarian café in the liveliest part of Gràcia offers a varied menu of salads, snacks, pasta dishes, pancakes, omelettes, tofu burgers, ice-cream and home-made cakes.

Mesopotamia
Carrer de Verdi 65. Tel: 93 237 1563. ££. This seriously trendy restaurant, run by an Iraqi professor of languages, serves contemporary Iraqi cuisine such as aubergines in yoghurt, courgettes with mint, chicken with rosewater and cardamom, and home-made Mesopotamian bread.

Roig Robí
Carrer de Sèneca 20. Tel: 93 218 9222. £££. Antoni Tàpies designed the menu at this smart modern Catalan restaurant, a popular haunt of politicians and artists. If you can afford to splash out, try the truffle-tasting menu, which includes *foie gras* with truffle jelly and truffle-stuffed squid.

Shojiro

Carrer de Ros de Olano 11. Tel: 93 415 6548. ££. The food at this hip modern bistro is a mix of Mediterranean and Japanese influences, with a daily changing selection of sashimi and Catalan meat and seafood dishes marinated in oriental-style sauces.

Cafés and bars

Hidden among Gràcia's narrow streets are several attractive squares, lined with open-air cafés and bars that come alive on summer evenings. The biggest buzz is usually around Plaça del Sol, whose sunny pavement cafés are also good for a daytime drink or snack. Among the options on this square are the ever-popular **Café del Sol** (*Plaça del Sol 16*), the Lebanese restaurant **Amir de Nit** (*Plaça del Sol 2*), and **Sol Solet** (*Plaça del Sol 13*), a lively *tapas* bar which at night serves unusual wholefood *tapas* such as couscous, Greek salad and quiches. Just off the square, **Tetería Jazmin** (*Carrer Maspons 11*) is a cool Moroccan-style tearoom, with low stools, sofas and hanging carpets, and mint tea served in copper pots.

Shopping

Avinguda Diagonal, between Gràcia and Pedralbes, is Barcelona's premier business and commercial district. The shops here have none of the charm or eccentricity of those in the older parts of town, but they are still a good choice if you are after household names and global fashion brands. There are branches of the department store **El Corte Inglés** at Plaça Francesc Macià and Plaça Reina Maria Cristina, and a huge modern shopping mall, **L'Illa Diagonal** (*Avinguda Diagonal 557*), with top names in fashion and cosmetics, toy shops including Imaginarium and the Disney Store, and specialist food stalls in the basement. Unusually, this area is not served by the Metro, but a special shoppers' bus service, known as **TombBus**, runs along the Diagonal and continues to Plaça de Catalunya every few minutes between Monday and Saturday.

FC Barcelona

The slogan 'mes que un club' *has real meaning when applied to FC Barcelona. Barça, as everybody calls it, is indeed so much more than a football club – it is an enduring symbol of Catalan pride.*

Throughout its hundred-year history, the club has been used by supporters and opponents alike as a symbol of Catalan nationalism. During the Franco dictatorship, when matches were rigged and the Catalan flag was banned, supporters would fill the Camp Nou with the scarlet-and-blue flags of Barça in the one gesture of Catalan solidarity they were allowed. When Josep Tarradellas returned from exile in 1977, his first appearance at the ground turned into a political rally, with supporters chanting '*Visca Barça! Visca Catalunya!*' ('Long live Barça! Long live Catalonia!'). Even today, matches against arch-rivals Real Madrid are hyped weeks in advance and turned into a battle between the region and the country. For immigrants to Barcelona, becoming a *cule* (a Barça fan) is still the most important way of establishing a Catalan identity.

The **Museu del Futbol Club Barcelona** (*open: Mon–Sat 1000–1830, Sun 1000–1400 depending on games; ££*) tells the history of the club, founded in 1899 by a group of foreign businessmen. There are also photos of legendary players,

from Pepe Samitier and Ladislao Kubala through to more recent foreign stars such as Cruyff, Maradona, Lineker and Ronaldo. It was Cruyff who inspired Barça's most famous victory, a 5–0 win at Real Madrid in the dying days of the Franco dictatorship, and who later became their most successful manager of all time, winning four successive Spanish championships and the 1992 European Cup.

The Camp Nou stadium (*Avinguda Arístides Maillol; tel: 93 496 3600; Metro: Collblanc*), which opened in 1957, can hold 120,000 spectators – the largest in Europe and the second largest in the world. If you can, get to a game here to experience the passion and pride many people feel in being Catalan. Access to the museum and shop is through gate 9; the ticket office (*open: Mon–Fri 1000–1300, 1600–2000; tickets usually go on sale around two days before each match*) is at gate 15, and most Spanish league games take place on Sunday afternoons between September and June. Any spare tickets are sold from 1100 outside gates 4 and 18.

" *People were raising their children up to our windows, old ladies were on their knees. It was incredible, as if we were the triumphant army that had returned ... It brought home to me that the suffering of the past was something that had stuck these people together, through generations. I felt it had nothing to do with sport at all.* "

Terry Venables, manager of Barça 1984–7, on winning the championship, quoted in Jimmy Burns, *Barça: A People's Passion*, 1999

EXCURSIONS

Excursions

Among the attractions within easy reach of Barcelona are a pair of historic cities, Catalonia's most sacred site and the beaches of the Costa Brava and Costa Daurada.

147

BEST OF

Excursions

Getting there: RENFE train services to other parts of Catalonia depart from Estació de Sants, reached by Metro to Sants-Estació. Many of the services also stop at Passeig de Gràcia, closer to the city centre. The Catalan government has its own suburban train network, Ferrocarrils Generalitat de Catalunya (FGC), with services to Montserrat. Buses to other parts of Catalonia depart from Estació del Nord, close to Arc de Triomf Metro station.

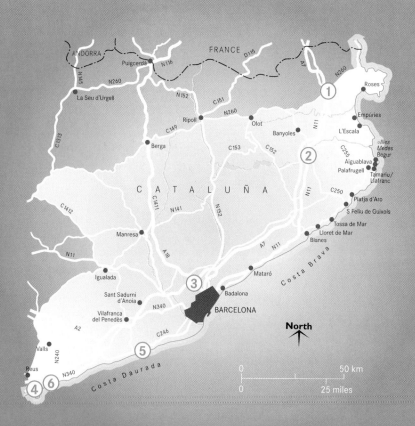

① Figueres

This county town close to the French border is best known as the birthplace of the surrealist painter **Salvador Dalí**, whose bizarre 'theatre-museum', designed by the artist as his own memorial, is a surreal experience in itself. **Pages 150–1**

② Girona

Girona has been described as a miniature Barcelona, with all the style of the Catalan capital but small enough to explore in a day. The old town, on the right bank of the Onyar river, contains at its heart one of the **best-preserved Jewish quarters** in Spain. **Pages 152–3**

③ Montserrat

The spiritual centre of Catalonia has been a place of pilgrimage for more than a thousand years, and a refuge of Catalan nationalism during periods of repression. The journey there, on a cable-car ride up the mountainside, is as exhilarating as the monastery itself. **Pages 154–5**

④ Port Aventura

Thrills of a different kind are on offer at **Spain's premier theme park**, whose attractions include one of the biggest roller-coasters in the world. Conveniently located close to the beaches of the Costa Daurada, this is an essential day out for families with children. **Pages 156–7**

⑤ Sitges

Until the creation of new beaches beside the Olympic port, this was where the people of Barcelona came for a day out by the sea. The old-fashioned resort retains a great deal of its charm, and has also developed a reputation as the **gay capital** of mainland Spain. **Page 159**

⑥ Tarragona

When the Romans invaded Spain, they made Tarragona the capital of their western Mediterranean empire. There are still a number of **Roman remains** dotted around the city, including an amphitheatre, a necropolis and the site of the old circus. **Pages 160–1**

Tip

If you plan on doing several excursions, or visiting the Costa Brava, it may be worth hiring a car. Driving and parking in central Barcelona is such a nightmare that the best bet is usually to collect your car from the airport, using local transport (see page 182) to get there. The major international car rental companies all have offices at the airport; one of the best is Europcar (tel: 93 298 3300). To hire a car, you must be over 21, and you will need your passport, driving licence and credit card.

Figueres

RENFE trains from Estació de Sants or Passeig de Gràcia (1 hr 45 mins). Tourist office: Plaça del Sol, tel: 972 503155.

The county town of the Upper Empordà region has been put on the map by the surrealist artist **Salvador Dalí**, who was born here in 1904. Dalí had his first exhibition in the town's opera house, now the **Teatre-Museu Dalí** (*Plaça Gala-Salvador Dalí; tel: 972 677500, www.dali-estate.org; open: Oct–June, Tue–Sat 1030–1715; July–Sept, 0900–1915 daily; ££*), the most visited museum in Catalonia and one of the three most visited in Spain. The name does not just reflect the fact that the building was once a theatre; it was consciously designed by Dalí as a **surrealist experience**, with the 'audience' free to create their own reactions without the distractions of captions, catalogues or guided tours. Such considerations have now been set aside, but the best way to explore is still to do as Dalí wished and allow your senses to guide you around a museum where nothing is quite as it seems.

From the outside of the building, with its trademark Daliesque eggs and bread rolls sculpted out of plaster, it is clear that Dalí enjoyed playing tricks on his visitors. A pink sofa turns into the lips of Mae West; a taxi in the courtyard, topped by

tractor tyres and an old fishing boat, sprays water over its inhabitants when a coin is fed into the slot. In the central auditorium, beneath a huge glass dome, a portrait of Dalí's wife Gala is enigmatically entitled *Gala Nude Looking at the Sea, Which at a Distance of Eighteen Metres is Transformed into a Portrait of Abraham Lincoln.*

But among the jokes and illusions are some remarkable paintings that give a real insight into Dalí's troubled mind. In particular, look out for two very different self-portraits: *Self-Portrait with L'Humanité*, painted in 1923, a statement of communist sympathies which enraged his notary father, and *Soft Self-Portrait with Grilled Bacon*, produced in 1941 and typical of Dalí's later work. Other famous paintings include *The Spectre of Sex Appeal* and *The Apotheosis of the Dollar*, as well as a Dalí portrait of **Picasso** and an **El Greco** from Dalí's private collection.

Dalí spent the final years of his life as a recluse in a tower adjoining the museum, and he is buried in a crypt beneath the stage.

A short climb uphill from the museum leads to **Castell de Sant Ferran** (*Carrer de Sant Ferran; open: June–Sept, 1030–2000 daily; Oct–May, Tue–Fri 1030–1300, Sat–Sun 1030–1300, 1600–1800; £*), a star-shaped citadel which was the last bastion of republican forces during the Spanish Civil War. Back in town, a statue on the *rambla* pays tribute to Figueres' other famous son, the inventor of the submarine **Narcís Monturiol**. The nearby **Museu de l'Empordà** (*Rambla 2; open: Tue–Sat 1100–1900, Sun 1000–1400, closed Mon; £*) has a room devoted to Monturiol, while the charming **Museu del Joguet** (*Carrer Sant Pere 1; open: Tue–Sat 1000–1300, 1600–1900, Sun 1100–1330, closed Mon; ££*) is a toy museum featuring everything from toy soldiers and dolls' houses to a teddy bear belonging to Dalí's sister.

Girona

RENFE trains from Estació de Sants or Passeig de Gràcia (1 hr 15 mins). Tourist office: Rambla de la Llibertat 1, tel: 972 226575.

Of all Catalonia's provincial cities, Girona holds the most appeal. It is a thoroughly modern city, with trendy pavement cafés, a thriving arts scene, a large student population and a reputation for Catalan nationalism; but at the same time, it shelters a medieval quarter which is more than a match for Barcelona's Barri Gòtic. It is no surprise that Girona is referred to, not disparagingly, as 'Barcelona's little sister'.

The trains drop you in the Eixample, built in the early 20th century on the left bank of the Onyar river. As in Barcelona, the creation of the Eixample coincided with the rise of the Modernist movement, and there are several Modernist buildings by local architect Rafael Masó. Also on this side of town, Parc de la Devesa is Catalonia's largest urban park, the source of the plane trees on La Rambla in Barcelona.

The avenues of trees are planted so close that they have no way to grow but up, and have reached heights of more than 50m (165ft).

It takes about 15 minutes to walk to Pont de Pedra, the stone bridge over the Onyar where the old town meets the new. Pause here to admire the best-known image of Girona, the tenement houses on the *rambla* with their backs to the river, painted an assortment of oranges, ochres and pinks. From here you can plunge into the old town, with its narrow streets named after the medieval guilds – Carrer de l'Argenteria ('silversmiths'), Carrer Mercaders ('merchants'), Carrer Ferreries Velles ('blacksmiths'), Carrer Peixateries Velles ('fishmongers') – now lined with arty and old-fashioned shops.

At the heart of the old town, the Call Jueu was one of the largest Jewish quarters in Spain, numbering up to a thousand people before expulsion in 1492. It was here that Rabbi Nahmánides founded the Cabbalist school of mysticism, a story told at the Centre Bonastruc Ça Porta (*Carrer Sant Llorenç; open: Mon–Sat 1000–1800, Sun 1000–1400; £*), a Jewish museum and cultural centre. The dark streets of the Jewish ghetto around Carrer de la Força have recently been opened up, creating a hauntingly atmospheric streetscape where sunlight throws shadows on the golden stone and street lamps light the cobbled passageways after dark.

Near here, the Catedral (*open: 1000–1400, 1600–1800 daily; admission free*) is one of the most impressive Gothic churches in Spain, reached by a handsome baroque stairway. The single nave is the widest in Europe, and the cathedral museum, beside the cloisters, contains a vivid 11th-century tapestry of the Creation. The tourist office sells a combined entrance ticket to all of Girona's museums, which include the Banys Àrabs (*Carrer Ferran el Catòlic; open: Oct–Mar, Tue–Sun 1000–1400; Apr–Sept, Tue–Sat 1000–1900, Sun 1000–1400; £*), a restored 13th-century bath-house; the Museu Arqueològic (*Carrer Santa Llúcia 1; open: Tue–Sat 1000–1400, 1600–1800, Sun 1000–1400, closed Mon; £*), with Roman and Jewish artefacts in an old monastery; and the Museu d'Art (*Pujada de la Catedral 12; open: Tue–Sat 1000–1800, Sun 1000–1400, closed Mon; £, but free on Sun*) in the old bishop's palace, featuring Catalan art from the 10th to 20th centuries. For a pleasant walk, follow Passeig de la Muralla along the top of the medieval walls.

" I made my way through deserted squares surrounded by massive stone arcades. On I went, my footsteps echoing up cobbled ramps and flights of steps. Why, I wondered, a little panicky, was there not a soul about? "

Nicholas Woodsworth in Girona,
***Financial Times*, 1998**

Montserrat

FGC from Plaça d'Espanya to Aeri de Montserrat, followed by cable-car.
Tel: 93 877 7777.

If you make only one trip out of Barcelona, this should be the one. For nervous travellers there is the option of a direct bus from Sants railway station (*departure 0900 daily*), but the classic way to approach Montserrat is via a one-hour suburban train trip followed by a terrifying cable-car ride. As the cable-car swoops up the mountain with the monastery looming above and a sheer drop beneath, you really do feel that, like a true pilgrim, you are placing your life in the hands of God and the Virgin of Montserrat.

The saw-toothed mountain (Montserrat means 'serrated mountain') which stands guard over Barcelona has been a place of pilgrimage for more than a thousand years. The story goes that St Peter placed a statue of the Virgin, carved by St Luke, here after Christ's death. For many years the statue was hidden from the Moors, then in AD 880 it was rediscovered by shepherds who were led to a cave on the mountain by angelic voices and heavenly light. A chapel was built to house the statue, and pilgrims flocked to worship the **Black**

Madonna, known as *la moreneta* ('the little dark one'). The fact that the statue almost certainly dates from the 12th century does nothing to reduce the power of the legend.

Montserrat is the spiritual centre of Catalonia, the Virgin of Montserrat its most powerful symbol. She has given her name to a Caribbean island and to thousands of Catalan women, such as the opera singer Montserrat Caballé. During the Franco dictatorship, the monastery became a focus for Catalan nationalism, holding services in Catalan and providing a sanctuary for opponents of the régime. It was here in 1974 that a 75th anniversary celebration for FC Barcelona was used to launch the political party led by Jordi Pujol, in a mass rally which turned into a potent Catalan mix of politics, religion and football.

The main focus is the Basilica, a 16th-century Renaissance church with a 20th-century façade. Mass is held here at 1100 daily, and a boys' choir sings twice daily at 1300 and 1845. In a chapel behind the altar (*access 0800–1030 and 1200–1830 daily*), pilgrims queue to touch the Black Madonna, which sits on a silver throne embossed with the coat of arms of Catalonia. If you want to join in, the ritual is to kiss or touch the Virgin's right hand while opening out your other hand to the infant Jesus.

> " *Montserrat could only be in Catalonia ... it could exist nowhere else in Spain. Montserrat has a bounce and a gusto that is all Catalan. It is unmistakably Spain, but Spain, the Catalans would say, plus.* "
>
> **Jan Morris, *Spain*, 1964**

Outside the church, the Museu de Montserrat (*open: Mon–Fri 1000–1800, Sat–Sun 0930–1830; ££*) features paintings by El Greco, Casas, Rusiñol and Picasso as well as an exhibition on the iconography of the Virgin of Montserrat.

The hills around the monastery provide excellent walking in an area rich in fauna and flora. One easy walk is the descent to Santa Cova (*open: 1015–1630 daily*), a chapel inside the cave where the statue is said to have been discovered. A funicular railway takes you part of the way, then a footpath leads past sculptures by Gaudí and Puig i Cadafalch depicting the mysteries of the Rosary. More serious walkers can take the funicular to the upper station of Sant Joan, where a one-hour hike leads to the summit of Montserrat, with views stretching to the Pyrenees and far out to sea.

Port Aventura

RENFE trains from Estació de Sants or Passeig de Gràcia (1 hr 15 mins). Tel:
977 779090; www.portaventura.es. Open: Apr–Oct, 1000–2000 daily (mid-
June to mid-Sept, 1000–2400). £££, but free for children under five.

The second largest theme park in Europe opened in 1995 and
has been pulling in the crowds ever since, reviving the Costa
Daurada ('Golden Coast') in the process and contributing to
the demise of at least one Barcelona funfair. Cultural tourists
will scoff that it has little to do with Catalonia, but there is
no doubt that Port Aventura makes a great day out – especially
for the kids.

The park is divided into **five themed areas**, purporting to
represent China, Mexico, Polynesia, the Wild West and a
Mediterranean fishing village. Each of these areas contains
a mixture of children's activities, restaurants, shops, white-
knuckle rides and live shows that are always entertaining
if not terribly authentic. 'Far West', for example, features
a stunt show and American Indian dancing; 'Mediterrania'
has a Spanish-style fiesta with fireworks, jet-skis and kites.
Elsewhere in the park, you can see Chinese acrobats and
magicians, Polynesian dancers, can-can girls, Mexican
singers and ancient Mayan rituals. Be aware that these
shows are extremely popular, and you may have to start
queuing around 30 minutes in advance. You can pick up a
leaflet with all the day's show
times at the entrance to the park.

For most visitors, the main
attraction lies in the thrill rides,
especially the **Dragon Khan**
roller-coaster, the largest in
Europe with its eight 360-degree
loops. Other favourites include
Tutuki Splash in Polynesia, a
water-ride down the slopes of an
erupting volcano (be prepared to
get very wet); the **Stampida**
wooden roller-coaster in Far
West; and **Kon-Tiki Wave**, a
giant swingboat which induces
definite feelings of queasiness as
it hovers above the water. There

Dragon Khan

Total length:
1 285m (4 215ft)
Maximum speed:
110km/h (70mph)
G-force: 4

are canoe rides and junior roller-coasters for younger kids, and plenty of safe play areas for toddlers. The latest attraction, introduced in 2000 by the park's new owners, Universal Studios, is **Sea Odyssey**, a simulated underwater journey with graphic computer animations of sea monsters, shipwrecks and marine life. Cartoon characters such as Woody Woodpecker, Rocky the Squirrel and Bullwinkle the Moose stroll around the park, delighting children and driving adults to distraction.

Port Aventura is so popular that it even has its own railway station, with frequent links to Barcelona. It is situated just outside the Costa Daurada resort of **Salou**, a huge summer playground with burger bars, discos and foreign pubs satisfying the tastes of visitors from all over Europe. The long sandy beach is backed by an attractive palm-lined promenade, where a statue recalls the conquest of Mallorca by Jaume I of Aragón, who sailed from Salou in 1229. Boats leave from the harbour several times a day in summer to **Cambrils**, a quieter resort which retains its fishing-village atmosphere, with pine-shaded beaches, a daily fish auction by the harbour and several excellent seafood restaurants.

157

Tips

● Waiting times for the most popular rides are posted at various noticeboards around the park. The queues are usually shorter at lunchtime and late in the day.
● If you don't have time to do everything in one day, you can convert your ticket into a two-day pass for a small additional fee – but you do have to return the very next day.

Sant Sadurni d'Anoia

RENFE trains from Estació de Sants or Plaça de Catalunya (45 mins).

This small town is the centre of production for Cava, the Catalan sparkling wine made by the same method as champagne. Cava owes its origins to the phylloxera plague of the late 19th century, which devastated the Catalan vineyards and forced winemakers into experimentation. The first bottle was produced in 1872 by **Josep Raventós**, heir to the Codorniu wine dynasty; there are now more than a

hundred cellars in the town, turning out 90 per cent of Spain's entire output of Cava.

The biggest name in Cava is still **Codorniu** (*Avinguda de Codorniu; tel: 93 818 3232; open: Mon–Fri 0900–1700, Sat–Sun 0900–1300; free guided tours, reservations advised*), which is worth a visit if only to see the vast Modernist wine cellars designed by **Puig i Cadafalch**. The tour includes a thrilling ride through the underground cellars, as well as a tasting and a thorough explanation of the production process. Premium Codorniu brands include **Ne Plus Ultra**, made with traditional Catalan grape varieties, and **Anna de Codorniu**, made with Chardonnay grapes. Their chief rivals are **Freixenet** (*Carrer Joan Sala 2; tel: 93 891 7000; open: Mon–Thu 0930–1130, 1530–1700, Fri 0930–1130, closed at weekends; free guided tours, reservations advised*), the world's biggest exporters of sparkling wine, conveniently situated beside the railway station. The Freixenet Christmas commercial is a Spanish institution and the tour includes a video of the most famous advertisements of the past, starring, among others, Montserrat Caballé, Raquel Welch and Sharon Stone.

Just down the railway line, **Vilafranca del Penedès** is the capital of the Penedès wine-producing district. The **Museu de Vilafranca** (*Plaça Jaume I; open: Tue–Sat 1000–1400, 1600–1900, Sun 1000–1400, closed Mon; £*) contains its very own wine museum, with winemaking equipment dating back to Roman times.

Sitges

RENFE trains from Estació de Sants or Passeig de Gràcia (30 mins). Tourist office: Carrer Sinia Morera 1, tel: 93 894 4251.

This cosmopolitan, low-rise beach resort has long attracted a different kind of tourist, ever since it became the meeting-place for a group of Modernist painters in the late 19th century. Artists still come, day-trippers flock here from Barcelona at weekends and gay tourists are drawn by its tolerant lifestyle – especially in February, when Rio comes to Catalonia with extravagant carnival parades and outrageous costumes.

Tip

Codorniu alone has more than 200,000 square metres of underground cellars, producing 30 million bottles of Cava each year, 75 per cent of which is consumed within Spain. One of their biggest customers is the Spanish royal family.

The setting is perfect: a succession of small beaches joined by a long promenade, beneath a rocky bluff overlooking the harbour. On the cliffs, the former home of the painter Santiago Rusiñol is now the Museu Cau Ferrat (*Carrer Fonollar; open: Tue–Sun 1000–1400, 1700–2100 in summer, Tue–Fri 1000–1330, 1500–1830, Sat 1000–1900, Sun 1000–1500 in winter; £*), with a remarkable collection of wrought iron and paintings by El Greco, Picasso and Rusiñol himself. Next door, the Museu Maricel (*open same hours; £*) includes Romanesque frescos, Gothic paintings and Catalan Modernist art, as well as apocalyptic murals by the war artist Josep Maria Sert. A belvedere features modern Catalan sculpture in a lovely setting, with picture windows looking out to sea.

Behind the headland is the oldest part of town, with narrow streets, whitewashed cottages, flower-filled balconies and chic boutiques and bars.

Tarragona

RENFE trains from Estació de Sants or Passeig de Gràcia (1 hr). Tourist office: Carrer Major 39, tel: 977 245203.

What is now a modern city of boulevards and ring roads was once imperial *Tarraco*, the capital of Rome's western Mediterranean empire. **Pontius Pilate** was born here, and **Julius Caesar** was one of many emperors to visit. Despite its proximity to the Costa Daurada beaches, Tarragona remains surprisingly off the tourist trail, especially when you consider that it contains some of the best-preserved **Roman remains** in Spain.

Most visitors from Barcelona will arrive at the railway station, situated on the seafront a kilometre (two-thirds of a mile) from the centre. Near here is **El Serralló**, the charming fishermen's quarter, where smacks are tied up around the harbour and fishermen sit in the sun mending their nets. There are several good seafood restaurants and *tapas* bars down by the water's edge.

Following the waterfront from the station to the city centre, you soon reach the foot of Rambla Nova, an attractive promenade lined with cafés, florists and shops. A mirador close by looks down over the **Amfiteatre Romà** (*open: Oct–June, Tue–Sat 1000–1330, 1530–1730, Sun 1000–1400, closed Mon; July–Sept, Tue–Sat 0900–2100, Sun 0900–1500, closed Mon; £*), built into the hillside in the 2nd century AD. Once the venue for gladiatorial contests and the martyrdom of Christians, these days it is a peaceful arena overlooking the sea, with the remains of a Romanesque church at its centre.

Above the amphitheatre, the oldest part of Tarragona is still enclosed within its Roman walls, now the base for a pleasant walk along the **Passeig Arqueològic** (*access from Via de l'Imperi Romà; same hours as amphitheatre; £*). The streets of the old town lead up towards the **Catedral** (*Plaça de la Seu; open: mid-Mar to mid-Nov, Mon–Sat 1000–1300,*

*1600–1900; mid-Nov to mid-Mar, 1000–1400, closed Sun;
£*), built between the 12th and 14th centuries on the site of
a Roman temple in a mix of Romanesque and Gothic styles.
The **cloister** here, with a garden of orange trees at the
centre, is particularly attractive. Also in the old town, the
Museu Nacional Arqueològic de Tarragona (*Plaça del
Rei; open: Oct–May, Tue–Sat 1000–1330, 1600–1900, Sun
1000–1400, closed Mon; June–Sept, Tue–Sat 1000–2000,
Sun 1000–1400, closed Mon; £*) features Roman pottery
and coins, and an outstanding collection of **Roman mosaics**,
while the nearby **Circ-Pretori** (*Plaça del Rei; same hours
as amphitheatre; £*) is a branch of the city history museum
which incorporates parts of the Roman *praetorium* ('governor's
residence') and a circus where chariot races were held. Climb
up to the tower, built in the 1st century AD, for good views
over the city.

On the way back to the station, you could take a diversion
past the **Forum Romà** (*Carrer de Lleida; same hours as
amphitheatre; £*), the old Roman forum outside the city
walls which was the centre of political and commercial
life. A walk of about a kilometre leads to the **Museu i
Necròpolis Paleocristiana** (*Avinguda Ramon i Cajal;
same hours as Museu Nacional Arqueològic and entered on
same ticket*), a late Roman burial ground on the banks of
the Francolí river. Finally, if you have a car, don't miss the

Pont de les Ferreres, a magnificent
Roman aqueduct 4km (2 $\frac{1}{2}$ miles)
north of Tarragona, visible from the
A7 motorway but best reached by
taking the N240 towards Valls.

Tip

*Most of Tarragona's museums
and Roman sites (but not the
archaeological museum) can
be visited on a combined ticket,
available from the tourist office
or any of the sites. Remember
that all of them are closed
on Mondays.*

The Costa Brava

We're taking the Costa Brava plane,
Y viva España.

When tourists started visiting the Spanish *costas* in the 1950s and 1960s, they came to the Costa Brava. This small corner of Catalonia, from Blanes to the French border, was used by the Franco government as a testing-ground for mass tourism, with tourist offices set up all over Europe to

> *Between the sea and the little creeks of white sand and the shadowing pines and the paths that climb the wooded mountainside, the mellow days slide like sun-warmed apricots that burst with ripeness, the nights ... must surely be like purple figs.* "

Rose Macaulay,
Fabled Shore, **1949**

promote the Costa Brava as a sun-and-sea destination. The travel writer Norman Lewis, who spent three years working as a fisherman in a Costa Brava village, has described in his memoir *Voices of the Old Sea* how the coastline was ravaged and the old way of life destroyed in the frantic desire to make a quick buck out of package tourism.

More than five million foreign tourists visit the Costa Brava every year. Most of them stay in the mega-resorts to the south, such as Lloret de Mar and Platja d'Aro, both of which throb all summer long with all-night discos and bronzed bodies on the beach. Even at this crowded southern end of the *costa*, there are still attractive spots, such as Blanes, a busy resort but also a working fishing port, and Tossa de Mar, where the fortified walls of the medieval town stand guard over the beach.

The real Costa Brava begins further north, in the bays and coves around the market towns of Begur and Palafrugell. It was places like Aiguablava, Llafranc and Tamariu, with their rocky shorelines, crescent beaches and pine-scented creeks, that the journalist Ferran Agulló had in mind when he labelled this the Costa Brava ('Wild Coast') in 1908. These places are no strangers to tourism, but the tourists who come here are of a more discerning nature, many of them second-home owners from Barcelona. They are just as likely to be interested in scuba-diving off the Illes Medes or Greek and Roman archaeology at Empúries as in the fleshpots of Platja d'Aro to the south.

163

There is a train service from Barcelona to Blanes in summer, and boats leave from Blanes to the various Costa Brava resorts. There are also regular buses to towns on the Costa Brava from Barcelona's Estació del Nord. However, to get the most out of this area, you really need a car. Take the A7 motorway north towards Girona and then follow one of the side roads down to the coast.

Lifestyles

Shopping, eating, children and nightlife in Barcelona

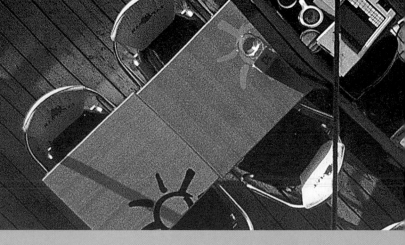

LIFESTYLES

Shopping

Shopping in Barcelona reflects the city itself – an enticing blend of fashion and tradition. There are up-to-the-minute shopping malls selling the latest designs alongside neighbourhood markets and quirky, old-fashioned shops. What they all have in common is a certain sense of style, which has made Barcelona one of the style capitals of Europe.

Most shops are open Monday to Saturday from around 1000 to 1400 and 1630 to 2000. Some shops close on Saturday afternoons, especially in summer, though this custom is gradually dying out. The tradition of taking a lunchtime siesta is still very much alive, though this too is under threat from the growing number of department stores and shopping malls which open from 1000 to 2130 six days a week. The majority of shops are closed on Sundays, except during the run-up to Christmas. The exception is the **Maremagnum** mall at Port Vell, open from 1100 to 2300 every day of the year.

The prices on display generally include a sales tax (IVA) of 16 per cent. Visitors from European Union countries must pay this tax, but are exempt from customs duty on their return home. Travellers from non-EU countries may claim a tax rebate on purchases above a set limit, currently 15,000 pesetas. This is usually given in the form of a cheque at customs, but if you shop at a store displaying the 'Tax Free Shopping' logo you may be able to claim an immediate refund on your credit card. If you are looking for bargains, many stores hold their annual sales (*rebajas*) in late January and February, and again in July and August.

Where to shop

The tourist office has created a **Barcelona Shopping Line**, a 5km (3-mile) route through the main shopping districts of the city. It starts at Maremagnum on the waterfront, continues up La Rambla and Passeig de Gràcia, then turns left along Avinguda Diagonal as far as Plaça Reina Maria Cristina. A

number of shops along this route display the Barcelona Shopping Line logo, which acts as a guarantee of quality. Although it would be unadventurous to follow this route precisely, it makes a good starting-point for a shopping tour of the city. As a general rule, the smart shops and fashion emporiums are found on Passeig de Gràcia and Avinguda Diagonal, while the small, specialist shops are hidden away in the back streets of the Barri Gòtic, El Born and El Raval.

Department stores and malls

Spain's biggest and best-known department store, **El Corte Inglés**, has four branches in Barcelona. The largest branch is on Plaça de Catalunya, with four floors of fashions and two floors of home furnishings, as well as toys, electronic equipment and a supermarket and delicatessen in the basement. There are two more branches on Avinguda Diagonal, and another specialising in books, music and sports equipment on Avinguda Portal de l'Angel. The

Plaça de Catalunya branch now has a competitor in the British giant **Marks & Spencer**, whose flagship Spanish store sits just across the square.

The best of the shopping malls is **L'Illa** (*Avinguda Diagonal 557*), a 'horizontal skyscraper' designed by Rafael Moneo in Barcelona's most upmarket commercial district. There are over a hundred shops here on three different levels, including such high-street fashion names as Benetton, Lacoste, Mango and Zara. A market in the basement contains speciality food stalls. Not far from here, **Pedralbes Centre** (*Avinguda Diagonal 609*) is another modern mall with a range of sophisticated boutiques. **El Triangle** (*Plaça de Catalunya*) features shoes from Camper and clothes from Massimo Dutti, as well as the interior design shop Habitat and a Fnac book megastore, while **Maremagnum** (*Moll d'Espanya*) is good for souvenirs, including FC Barcelona outfits and merchandise at the club shop La Botiga del Barça. The biggest mall of all, **Barcelona Glòries** (*Avinguda Diagonal 208; Metro: Glòries*), is somewhat out of the way but can be combined with a trip to Els Encants flea market (*see page 169*). More appealing are the *galerias* ('shopping arcades') in the city centre, such as **Bulevard Rosa** (*Passeig de Gràcia 55*) for fashions and its neighbour **Bulevard dels Antiquaris** for antiques.

Markets and flea markets

Every district of Barcelona has its own covered market, many based in handsome 19th-century buildings. They are generally open Monday to Saturday from around 0800 to 1400, and sometimes in the evenings too. **La Boqueria** on La Rambla is open throughout the day, with stalls selling meat, fish, cheese, ham, olives, fresh produce, dried fruit and nuts. Other good markets are **Mercat de Sant Antoni** on the edge of the Raval and **Mercat de la Llibertat** in Gràcia, which retains its villagey atmosphere. **Mercat de la Concepció** (*Carrer*

de València) in the Eixample is famous for its flower displays. An artesan food market is held twice a month on Plaça del Pi (*see page 58*), when small producers display honey, fig cake, organic bread and farmhouse cheeses at outdoor stalls on the square.

Artists set up stall in Plaça Sant Josep Oriol at weekends, and there are antique and craft stalls outside the cathedral on Thursdays. For a bit of browsing, it can be fun to visit one of Barcelona's various second-hand markets. Books and coins are sold outside Mercat de Sant Antoni on Sunday mornings, when a stamp and coin market also takes place in Plaça Reial. Also at weekends, a bric-à-brac market is set up on the quay at the foot of La Rambla, with stalls selling pottery, costume jewellery, vintage clothing and

antiques. For a taste of old Barcelona, head for **Els Encants** (*Plaça de les Glòries Catalanes; Metro: Glòries; open: Mon, Wed, Fri, Sat 0900–1900*), a genuine flea market where you might pick up a bargain among the heaps of walking sticks, wind-up gramophones, porn videos and second-hand furniture.

What to buy

Art and design: Even the tourist souvenirs are tasteful in Barcelona, and most people come home with a Miró mug or Picasso T-shirt from one of the museum shops. For the best in contemporary Catalan design, visit the **Centre Català d'Artesania** on Passeig de Gràcia, or the design guru **Vinçon** on the same street.

Ceramics: Spanish pottery is always good value and ranges from elaborate Moorish designs to simple brown-glazed cooking pots. A huge selection from all over Spain is on sale at **Art Escudellers** (*Carrer dels Escudellers 23*).

Fashions: Look out for clothes by top Spanish and Catalan designers, such as **Adolfo Domínguez** (*Passeig de Gràcia 32*) and **Antonio Miró** (*Carrer Consell de Cent 349*). The most upmarket fashion stores are found on Passeig de Gràcia and in the area around Plaça de Francesc Macià on Avinguda Diagonal, while clubwear and alternative street fashions are sold on Carrer Portaferrissa in the Gothic Quarter and Carrer Riera Baixa in El Raval.

Leather and shoes: Spanish leather is no longer the bargain it was, but the quality is good and prices are reasonable if you shop around. The best-known store is **Loewe** (*Passeig de Gràcia 35*), but for sturdy footwear from sandals to riding boots it is hard to beat **Sole** (*Carrer Ample 7*).

Music: Shops like **Fnac** and **El Corte Inglés** have a huge range of CDs featuring *sardanas*, flamenco and contemporary Spanish rock, as well as Cuban and Latin American dance music at reasonable prices.

169

Eating out

*The cooking of Spain is regional cuisine, rooted in the landscape and history of the various regions. Catalonia in particular has its own **rich culinary tradition**, based on the produce of the mountains and the sea. Most restaurants in Barcelona serve Catalan cooking, though there are others specialising in Basque, Galician, Castilian or Riojan cuisine. Immigration has brought a proliferation of Indian, Japanese and Middle Eastern restaurants, and the latest trend to emerge is a 'modern Catalan' style of cooking, where classic regional dishes are reinvented with Italian or Japanese touches.*

The lateness of Spanish mealtimes comes as a shock to visitors from northern Europe and America. **Breakfast** is a casual affair, usually a milky coffee and a croissant or sandwich at any time up to about 1200. Very few restaurants serve **lunch** before 1300 or **dinner** before 2100, and it is quite normal to see people sitting down to dinner at 2300, especially at weekends. Other than eating in *tapas* bars, there is very little you can do about this, so you may as well just get used to it.

Most restaurants serve a *menú del dia* ('menu of the day') at lunchtime, a set three- or four-course meal with house wine or water included – great value if you are on a budget. A few places serve a *menú* in the evenings too, but eating out at night is generally more expensive. Although reservations are not usually essential, it is always a good idea to book a table, especially on Friday and Saturday nights, or for Sunday lunch. Most restaurants are closed on Sunday evenings.

COMESTIBLES
FINOS
IMPORTACIÓN
DIRECTA
DE LAS PRIMERAS
MARCAS MUNDIALES

Formal dress is not necessary except at the very smartest restaurants, but the Catalans do like to look their best and smart casual dress is the norm. Children are welcome in all

but the most formal establishments; there is rarely a special children's menu, but most places will serve half-portions on request. Vegetarians could have a hard time, as even innocuous-sounding salads tend to appear with pieces of meat and fish and you don't want to rely on *tortilla* (potato omelette) for every meal. Besides the handful of vegetarian restaurants, a welcome recent trend has been the appearance of vegetarian options alongside more traditional choices. This is particularly true of the trendier restaurants in areas such as **Gràcia**, **El Raval** and **El Born**.

Catalan cuisine

Traditional Catalan cooking is not for the squeamish, with its heavy reliance on seafood, game and offal. The most characteristic style is known as *mar i muntanya* ('sea and mountain'), mixing the products of land and sea to produce unlikely combinations such as chicken with lobster, pig's trotters with prawns, or a ragout of rabbit, snails and seafood. One famous dish consists of

squid stuffed with minced pork in a chocolate sauce.

Fresh seafood is always a good choice, especially in the fish restaurants of **Barceloneta** and the **Olympic port**. Lobster, prawns and sole are all widely available, and can be combined in the seafood stew known as *sarsuela*. Another classic dish is *suquet de peix*, a casserole of white fish, potatoes and tomatoes. Paella comes from Valencia, but is available everywhere; the Catalan equivalents are *arròs negre* ('black rice', blackened with squid ink) and *fideuà*, based on noodles rather than rice.

171

Meat (beef, lamb or duck) is often cooked *a la brasa*, charcoal-grilled and accompanied by *allioli* (garlic mayonnaise). Such rustic grill-restaurants also specialise in *torrades*, a toasted version of the classic Catalan comfort food *pa amb tomàquet*, which is crusty bread rubbed with tomato and sprinkled with salt and olive oil. You can ask for this to be topped with *escalivada*, a cold dish of roasted peppers and aubergines. Another speciality, available only in spring, is *calçots*, spring onions the size of leeks grilled until they are black and dipped into a *romesco* sauce made with almonds, hazelnuts, tomatoes and garlic.

Desserts are not Spain's strong point, but Catalonia produces two of the best. *Crema catalana* is virtually the national dish, a rich egg custard with a burnt sugar crust, while *mel i mató* is a surprisingly successful combination of curd cheese with honey.

Catalan specialities

ànec amb peres
stewed duck with pears
bacallà a la llauna
baked salt cod with garlic, tomatoes and white wine
botifarra amb mongetes
Catalan sausage with white beans
cargols a la llauna
baked snails with *allioli*
espinacs a la catalana
spinach with pine nuts and raisins
sípia amb mandonguilles
cuttlefish with meatballs

Tapas and bar snacks

Tapas have their origins in the old Spanish custom of placing a free *tapa* ('lid'), such as a slice of ham or saucer of olives, over a drink. There is no tradition of *tapas* in Barcelona, but over the last few years there has been an explosion of *tapas* bars, particularly down by the **waterfront** and along **Passeig de Gràcia**. Some places have a menu; in others you simply point to what you want from the snacks displayed in a cabinet on the bar. Popular *tapas* include *tortilla* (potato omelette), *patatas bravas* (spicy potatoes), *gambas al ajillo* (garlic prawns) and *pulpo gallega* (octopus Galician-style).

A *tapa* is a small portion, a *racion* is larger, and you can ask for it to be served with *pa amb tomàquet*. Most bars also serve *bocadillos*, crusty bread rolls spread with tomato and filled with sausage, ham or cheese. An alternative to *tapas* is *pintxos*, the Basque-style titbits served at numerous bars in El Born (*see pages 74–5*). Although a selection of *tapas* can make a good substitute for an evening meal, the idea is simply to give you something to nibble during the early-evening cocktail hour before dinner.

Drinking

Most restaurants serve a good selection of Spanish and Catalan wines. The locals tend to drink red wine whatever they are eating, or occasionally rosé in summer. The top Spanish wines are the oak-aged reds from **Rioja** and **Ribera del Duero**, though Catalonia produces some excellent wines. Denominations to look out for include **Penedès**, **Costers del Segre** and **Priorat**, known for its serious, heavy red wines. As an introduction to Catalan wines, those made by **Torres** are always reliable; their single-estate Mas La Plana, made with Cabernet Sauvignon, has been favourably compared to the great red wines of Bordeaux. Cava, the sparkling wine

from the Penedès region, makes an inexpensive treat. It goes down well with early-evening *tapas*, as do *fino* (chilled dry sherry), *txakoli* (fizzy white wine from the Basque country) or *una canya*, a small glass of draught Spanish lager. Cocktails such as *gin-tonic* and *cuba-libre* (rum and Coke) are also popular, and meals are often finished off with a shot of Spanish brandy or an ice-cold fruit schnapps.

If you don't want to drink alcohol, the usual alternative is mineral water, though you will also see people ordering *gaseosa* (lemonade) and mixing it with cheap red wine. Another popular drink in summer is *granizado*, a fruit-juice slush with crushed ice, best enjoyed at a *granja*, a milk bar serving hot chocolate and cakes. **Coffee** is usually *café solo*, a small shot of espresso, or *cortado*, served with a dash of hot milk. The Catalans drink *café con leche* (milky coffee) for breakfast only, though you can ask for it at any time of day. For something less stimulating, finish your meal with a herbal infusion of *manzanilla* (camomile) or *menta* (mint).

173

Barcelona with children

Barcelona may feel like a grown-up city, but it is a great place for a holiday with kids. In fact, much of what makes Barcelona attractive to adults will appeal to children too.

Children love the street life on La Rambla, especially the **magicians** and **performance artists**; it is wonderful to watch a child's face when one of the statues springs to life. They are charmed by Gaudí's architecture and Miró's colourful designs, which remind them of the work they do at school. Most boys and quite a few girls want to visit the **Camp Nou**, to see the largest football stadium in Europe and come away with a Barça shirt, and there are few children who do not enjoy watching the *sardana dancers* outside the cathedral on

Sundays. On top of all that, there are lots of fun ways to get about, from open-top buses and boats to the Tibidabo tram.

The Spanish attitude to children is very different from northern Europe. Children are welcomed almost everywhere, but much of the time they are expected to behave like adults. Most **restaurants**, for example, will happily accept children, but there will be no allowance for their fussy dining habits and they will be expected to eat squid rings rather than fishfingers and chips. Special facilities, such as baby-changing rooms and pushchair ramps, are still extremely rare. On the other hand, all **parks** have children's play areas and a couple of them lay on special activities on Sunday mornings (*see below*). Many **museums** have hands-on activities and children's events at weekends, and the **beaches** are also child-friendly, with lifeguards, safe swimming, playgrounds and level promenades.

Family attractions

Aquàrium (*see page 92*)
The highlight of Barcelona's aquarium is a walk-through glass tunnel, where children can press

their faces up against the sharks. Younger children enjoy the touching pool for those touchy-feely experiences with sea creatures.

Font Màgica(see page 114) Children are enchanted by the *son et lumière* show at the 'magic fountain' on Plaça d'Espanya. The times vary throughout the year, but the show usually takes place on summer evenings, and occasionally on winter weekends.

Nits Hípiques *Pista d'Hípica La Foixarda, Avinguda dels Montanyans 1, Montjuïc.* Tourist offices sell tickets for this one-hour display of riding skills, performed on Friday evenings by the mounted unit of the municipal police force on their Spanish and Arab horses.

Tibidabo (see page 140). The ride up the mountainside on a vintage tram and funicular whets the appetite, and the amusement park at the summit is the icing on the cake for kids of all ages, from toddlers to grandparents.

Zoo de Barcelona (see page 91). Children always love a zoo, and this one is no exception. If elephants, gorillas, giant turtles and tropical birds are not enough, there are pony rides and a miniature train to keep them amused.

Parks

Barcelona's parks are great places for kids, with playgrounds and plenty of space to run about. **Turó Parc** (*Avinguda de Pau Casals*), near the Diagonal, has a theatre with puppet shows on Sunday mornings, while **Parc del Castell de l'Oreneta**, behind Pedralbes monastery, has a miniature steam train and pony rides on Sundays.

Shopping

Imaginarium is an enjoyable toy shop with branches across the city, easily recognised by their bright colours and toddler-size doorways for kids. They have branches in Maremagnum and L'Illa, where there is also a **Disney Store**. In the Barri Gòtic, **Joguines Foyé** (*Carrer Banys Nous 13*) is Barcelona's oldest toy shop, featuring toy soldiers, wooden horses and model cars and trains. Another traditional toy shop is **Joguines Monforte** (*Plaça Sant Josep Oriol 3*); near here are **Drap** (*Carrer del Pi 14*) for dolls' houses and furniture, and **Sardina Submarina** (*Carrer Cardenal Casañas 7*) for bright wooden toys. For budding magicians, take them to **El Ingenio** (*see page 61*) or **El Rei de la Màgia** (*see page 77*) and you will have made a friend for life.

175

After dark

Barcelona has a well-deserved reputation as a party city, where nightlife means what it says. The afternoon siesta has given most Spaniards a phenomenal amount of energy and the ability to stay up long after most sensible people have gone to bed. Theatre and cinema productions rarely start before 2200, jazz concerts kick off at midnight, and clubs start to fill up around 0100 and stay busy until breakfast time. Exhausted foreign tourists stumble back to their hotels at midnight wondering what all the fuss was about, then realise to their horror that they simply went out too early.

Information and tickets

For music, drama and cinema, you can find out what's on by looking in **local newspapers**, *Guía del Ocio* or the monthly English-language *Barcelona Metropolitan*. The city council also has full listings and daily recommendations in English on its website (*www.bcn.es*). Other sources of information are the tourist office on Plaça de Catalunya and the arts information and ticket office at Palau de la Virreina (*Rambla 99*).

Advance ticket sales are handled by branches of the two biggest savings banks, Caixa de Catalunya and Caixa de Pensions, though these rarely sell tickets for the same events. Caixa de Catalunya has a ticket desk inside the main tourist office, which often has standby tickets at half price three hours before a performance. Unfortunately, the rivalry between city and Catalan governments spills over into the arts sphere, making each reluctant to publicise the other's events; if you ask at the tourist office you can expect to be given information about city-sponsored arts companies only. If you know what you want to see, simply go to the box office of the relevant theatre.

Bars and clubs

The distinction between bars and clubs is blurred in Barcelona, with few places charging admission even at weekends and many bars turning into discos after midnight. The late-night scene is constantly on the move, and fashions change from week to week, but certain trends have emerged in different parts of town.

The discos of the **Maremagnum complex** are one enormous teen party. The **Port Olímpic** draws a youngish, fashionable crowd. The **lower half of the Barri Gòtic**, around Carrer dels Escudellers and Plaça Reial, is grungy and slightly edgy, while the Barrio Chino lives on in a handful of old-time bars in the **Raval** (*see page 45*). **Northern Raval** and **Born** are seriously hip, with Manhattan-style lofts turned into cocktail bars and dancefloors, while the design bars of the **Eixample** continue to hold a retro appeal for a laid-back thirty-something crowd.

During the style-conscious 1980s, design bars were all the rage, and they still make an enjoyable night out if only because they are so very Barcelona. For some reason, the toilets were always an important feature of these bars, with clever little post-modern tricks like fluorescent urinals with mirrors and flashing lights. Don't say you haven't been warned! One of the oldest is **Nick Havanna** (*Carrer del Rosselló 208*), with banks of TV screens and a pendulum over the dancefloor; others nearby are **Velvet** (*Carrer de Balmes 161*), more like a bordello with its red velvet curtains, and **Zsa Zsa** (*Carrer del Rosselló 156*), where the walls are lined with mirrors and Turkish kilims. The most unusual is **La Fira** (*Carrer de Provença 171*), themed as a fairground and packed out at weekends with a young crowd who enjoy walking through the hall of mirrors and sipping their drinks in old dodgem cars and carousels. The ultimate design bar, **Torres de Avila**, is up on Montjuïc at the entrance to Poble Espanyol (*see page 113*).

177

For late-night dancing, **Otto Zutz** (*Carrer de Lincoln 15*) is a survivor of the 1980s in Gràcia, while **Nayandei** is the biggest of the terrace clubs on the rooftop of Maremagnum. For something a little different, **La Paloma** is an old-style dance-hall in the Raval (*see page 45*), and **Buena Vista** (*Carrer del Rosselló 217*) is Barcelona's top salsa club, with free lessons on Wednesdays and Thursdays and *animadores* (in-house dancing partners) at weekends. If you want to know which places are currently hot, check out the flyers and magazines in the record and clubwear shops on Carrer Riera Baixa in El Raval.

Cinema

The latest Hollywood blockbusters dubbed into Spanish, as well as contemporary Spanish films, are shown at **Cines Maremagnum** (*Moll d'Espanya; tel: 93 405 2222*), a multi-screen complex at Port Vell, where there is also a giant-screen **IMAX** cinema (*Moll d'Espanya; tel: 93 225 1111*) featuring 3D wildlife spectaculars. For foreign films in the original language, try **Icària** (*Carrer de Salvador Espriu 61; tel: 93 221 7585*) in the Vila Olímpica or the art-house cinema **Verdi** (*Carrer de Verdi 32; tel: 93 237 0516*) in Gràcia.

Classical music, opera and theatre

A concert at the **Liceu** (*see page 28*) or **Palau de la Música Catalana** (*see page 72*) is an unforgettable experience, and many people go for the social aspect as much as for the music. Barcelona has recently acquired two new performance spaces in the Glòries district, a run-down area that has been redeveloped as a centre for the arts. The **Teatre Nacional de Catalunya** (*Plaça de les Arts 1; tel: 93 306 5700*), in a classical-style temple by local architect Ricard Bofill, opened in 1997 as a showcase for Catalan theatre, while the neighbouring **Auditori** (*Carrer de Lepant 150; tel: 93 247 9300*), by Spanish architect Rafael Moneo, opened in 1999 as the new home of Barcelona's symphony orchestra. Barcelona's major theatres include the **Teatre Principal** (*Rambla 27; tel: 93 301 4750*) on La Rambla, and the **Mercat de les Flors** (*Carrer de Lleida 59; tel: 93 426 1875*) in a converted flower market beneath Montjuïc. This is one of the main venues for the **Festival del Grec** (*see page 109*), a celebration of the performing arts held between June and August each year. Look out too for festivals of early music (May) and contemporary music (October), as well as concerts in the city's churches and squares.

like the **Olympic Stadium**, **Palau Sant Jordi** and **Camp Nou**. Tickets are expensive and hard to come by, but keep a look out for posters advertising what's on. The best-known music club is **La Boîte** (*Avinguda Diagonal 477; tel: 93 319 1789*), with a nightly programme of live acts including blues, soul and African percussion. **Jamboree** (*Plaça Reial 17; tel: 93 301 7564*) was Barcelona's first jazz cellar, and also features hip-hop and groove, while **Harlem Jazz Club** (*Carrer Comtessa de Sobradiel 8; tel: 93 310 0755*) is an intimate Barri Gòtic venue with free admission, except at weekends. Some of these places feature *flamenc fusió*, a Catalan form of flamenco influenced by jazz and Latin rhythms. For original foot-stomping Andalusian flamenco, try the tourist-oriented dinner shows at **Cordobes** (*Rambla 35; tel: 93 317 6653*), **El Patio Andaluz** (*Carrer d'Aribau 242; tel: 93 209 3378*) and **Tablao de Carmen** (*Poble Espanyol; tel: 93 325 6895*), or the more authentic late-night *tablao* at **Tarantos** (*Plaça Reial 17; tel: 93 389 1661*).

Jazz, rock and flamenco

The big Spanish and international megastars feature Barcelona on their tours, playing at large-scale venues

179

Practical
information

PRACTICAL INFORMATION

Practical information

Airports

Barcelona's airport (*tel: 93 298 3838*) is situated 12km (7 1/2 miles) south of the city at El Prat de Llobregat. Of the **three terminals**, Terminals A and B are mostly used for international flights and Terminal C for Spanish domestic flights. Terminals A and B have a full range of facilities, including currency exchange, car hire and tourist information offices.

The quickest way into the city centre is by **taxi**, though this is expensive and not really necessary unless you have heavy luggage or are travelling to an out-of-the-way part of town. If you do take a taxi, ignore any drivers who approach you inside the airport and join the queue for a licensed cab instead. Fares are fixed, but there are supplements for extra luggage and for late-night or weekend travel.

There are also two reliable and cheap public transport alternatives. The **Aerobús** is a special bus service connecting the airport to Plaça de Catalunya, with departures every 15 minutes from around 0600 to 2400. The journey takes about 30 minutes, depending on traffic. The cheapest option of all is to take one of the **airport trains** from the station, which is reached by an overhead walkway between Terminals A and B. These leave every 30 minutes from around 0600 to 2230 and take 23 minutes to reach Plaça de Catalunya. The trains also stop at Estació de Sants, allowing a choice of connections to the Metro system.

In summer, there are charter flights from a number of European airports to Girona (Costa Brava) and Reus (Costa Daurada), both of which can also be used as entry points for Barcelona.

Climate

Barcelona's Mediterranean climate is one reason for its appeal, with guaranteed sunshine in summer and mild winter days when it is still normally warm enough to eat lunch out of doors by the sea. The **best time to visit** is in early summer (May–June), when the days are long and daytime temperatures rise to around 25°C. In July and August, the heat and humidity can be oppressive, and autumn

(Sept–Nov) brings heavy rainfall along with a drop in temperatures, though even in October it can reach a very pleasant 23°C. Winter (Dec–Feb) can be lovely, with crisp sunny days, but it can also be cold and damp. One hazard, which can strike at any time, is the *tramuntana*, a fierce north wind that lasts for days at a time and strikes fear into the hearts of sailors and fishermen.

Currency

Spain's currency is the **peseta (pta)**, issued in coins from 1 to 500 ptas and banknotes from 1 000 to 10,000 ptas. The one-peseta coin is rarely seen these days and most bills are rounded down to the nearest 5 ptas. On 1 July 2002, the peseta will be replaced by the **euro**, and it is already common to see prices displayed in both currencies. Euro coins and notes will be issued in January 2002, and this will be followed by a six-month period during which both pesetas and euros will be in circulation.

Major credit cards are widely accepted, and travellers' cheques and foreign currency can be changed at banks, exchange bureaus and hotels. You will need to show your passport when changing travellers' cheques. Cash can also be obtained from ATMs (automated teller machines) using your credit or debit card. Your bank will make a charge for this, but it may compare favourably with the commission charged by Spanish banks for changing foreign currency.

Customs regulations

Visitors arriving from other European Union countries may bring in any amount of goods provided they are for personal use and tax has already been paid. The limits for travellers arriving from outside the EU are 1 litre of spirits, 2 litres of wine, 200 cigarettes and 50g of perfume.

Electricity

Electrical appliances run on 220–225 volts AC, using standard European round-pinned plugs. Visitors from the UK will require an **adaptor** and US visitors may need a **transformer** for appliances operating on 100–120 volts. If you have forgotten to bring these, they are usually available from El Corte Inglés department stores.

183

Entry formalities

Citizens of European Union countries may visit Spain without restrictions, provided they hold a valid passport or national identity card. All other visitors require a passport. Citizens of the USA, Canada, Australia and New Zealand do not need a visa for visits of less than 90 days. Citizens of South Africa and some other countries require a visa, issued by their nearest Spanish embassy or consulate.

Health and insurance

There are no major health hazards in Spain, though it is important to ensure that you are covered by adequate health insurance. Citizens of European Union countries should take **form E111**, which entitles them to free basic health care within the Spanish social security system. In most cases it will be easier to use **private health insurance**, included on a comprehensive travel insurance policy along with cover for accidents, theft and personal liability. This is advisable for everybody and essential for visitors from outside the European Union.

The biggest health hazard is usually the **sun**. It is important to protect your skin with a strong sunscreen and to avoid the intense heat of the early afternoon, at least until your body has acclimatised. Drink plenty of water, and remember that small children are particularly vulnerable. Tap water is safe to drink, but mineral water is widely available.

Pharmacies can easily be identified by a large flashing red or green cross displayed on the street. Outside normal hours, a notice on the door of each pharmacy gives the address of the nearest duty chemist. Pharmacies that are open 24 hours a day include **Farmàcia Alvarez** (*Passeig de Gràcia 26*) and **Farmàcia Clapés** (*Rambla 98*). In an emergency, go to the casualty department ('Urgències') of the **Hospital Clínic** (*Carrer de Villarroel 170*), or call an ambulance on **061**.

Information

The main tourist information office is situated beneath **Plaça de Catalunya**. It is open from 0900 to 2100 every day of the year except 1 Jan and 25 Dec. As well as information, the services on offer include hotel reservations, currency exchange, Internet access and a gift shop. It can also deal with telephone enquiries (*tel: 906 301282 if calling within Spain; from outside Spain dial (34) 93 304 3421*) and maintains an up-to-date website (*www.barcelonaturisme.com*). There are branches in the **city hall** (*Plaça Sant Jaume; open: Mon–Sat 1000–2000, Sun 1000–1400*) and the **Sants railway station** (*open: Mon–Fri 0800–2000, Sat–Sun 0800–1400; July–Sept 0800–2000 daily*), offering

information only. The city government also has lots of useful information, with links in English, on its website (*www.bcn.es*).

The Catalan government has its own tourist office, with information on Barcelona and Catalonia, in **Palau Robert** (*Passeig de Gràcia 107; tel: 93 238 4000; open: Mon–Sat 1000–1900, Sun 1000–1400*).

During the summer, an information kiosk is set up outside the **Sagrada Família**, and multilingual 'red jacket' tourist officers patrol La Rambla and the Barri Gòtic in pairs in their distinctive red and white uniforms.

For information on the latest shows and exhibitions, consult the local media. Newspapers such as *La Vanguardia* and *El Periodico de Catalunya* have excellent listings sections, and even if you cannot read Spanish or Catalan, it is usually possible to flick through the papers in a bar and get an idea of what's on. *Guía del Ocio* is a weekly listings magazine in Spanish, with full restaurant listings as well as cinemas, theatres and concerts. It is available from the news-stands on La Rambla or online (*www.guiadelociobcn.es*). There are various English-language publications you can pick up free in hotels and bars, including the monthly *Barcelona Metropolitan*, aimed mainly at foreign residents. The city's arts information office at **Palau de la Virreina** (*Rambla 99; tel: 93 301 7775*) is also a good source of information and tickets for local events.

In the UK, the Spanish government tourist office (*22–3 Manchester Square, London W1M 5AP; tel: 020 7486 8077, www.tourspain.es*) can supply information and maps before your trip.

Maps

A detailed city map is on sale at tourist information offices. It is also worth getting hold of a **public transport map**, available free of charge from Metro stations and tourist offices.

Opening times

Shops are generally open Monday to Saturday from around 1000 to 1400 and 1630 to 2000, though many shops close on Saturday afternoons. The majority of shops are closed on Sundays. The larger department stores tend to stay open throughout the day from around 1000 to 2130 six days a week, and the Maremagnum shopping mall is open every day of the year from 1100 to 2300. **Markets** start around 0800 and are usually closed by 1400, though some of the larger markets reopen in the evenings, and the Boqueria on La Rambla is open throughout the day.

Banks are open Monday to Friday from around 0900 to 1400, and on Saturday mornings between October and April. Outside these hours, you can change money at hotels, private exchange bureaus or the branch of Caixa Catalunya inside the main tourist office. There are also out-of-hours currency exchange services at the airport and Sants railway station.

Post offices are open from around 0830 to 1400 Monday to Friday and 0930 to 1300 on Saturdays, though stamps can be bought at tobacconists' outside these times. The main post office on the corner of Via Laietana and Passeig de Colom is open Monday to Saturday 0830 to 2130 and on Sundays from 0830 to 1430.

Restaurants typically open for lunch at around 1300 and for dinner at 2100, though *tapas* bars and some restaurants are open throughout the day. Most restaurants are closed for one day a week, usually Sunday or Monday, and the majority are closed on Sunday evenings.

Museums are usually closed on Mondays and on Sunday afternoons, but check the hours of individual entries in this book.

Public holidays

In addition to the national holidays which are taken across Spain, there are others that apply only to Catalonia. The majority of shops, banks and offices will be closed on these days, and museums and public transport facilities tend to keep Sunday hours. If a holiday falls on a Saturday or Sunday, many businesses will close on the following Monday instead; if it falls on a Tuesday or Thursday, it is traditionally extended over a long weekend, a device known as a *pont*, or bridge.

The following are the main public holidays in Catalonia:

1 January	New Year's Day
6 January	Epiphany
Friday before Easter	Good Friday
Monday after Easter	Easter Monday
1 May	Labour Day
24 June	Feast of St John
15 August	Assumption of the Virgin
11 September	La Diada (Catalan National Day)
12 October	Dia de la Hispanidad (Spanish National Day)
1 November	All Saints' Day
6 December	Constitution Day
8 December	Feast of the Immaculate Conception
25–26 December	Christmas

In addition, the city of Barcelona can declare two extra public holidays, one of which is usually taken on 24 September for the feast of Our Lady of Mercy (*see page 62*).

Reading

Barcelona, by art historian Robert Hughes, is the standard work on the city. Published in 1992 during the build-up to the Olympic Games, this is a monumental piece of scholarship, but personal insights and quirky anecdotes ensure that it is also a pleasure to read. Although the book spans 2 000 years of history, its principal focus is on the Modernist period of the late 19th and early 20th centuries. Colm Tóibín's ***Homage to Barcelona*** (1990) was also published during the pre-Olympic boom and is a vivid, personal, enthusiastic account by an Irish journalist living in the city and swept up in its mood of post-Franco optimism.

Two of the best modern Catalan writers have both been translated into English. Manuel Vázquez Montalbán is a crime writer, communist, food writer and restaurateur whose *Barcelonas* (1990) is not only an entertaining social history but an impassioned diatribe against the reinvention of the city. His crime novels, such as *Murder on the Central Committee* and *An Olympic Death*, are set in Barcelona and feature the popular gourmet detective Pepe Carvalho. Another contemporary Catalan novelist, who like Montalbán writes in Spanish, is Eduardo Mendoza, whose *City of Marvels* (1986) captures the mood of Barcelona between the World Fairs of 1888 and 1929.

The Catalan passion for food and football is explored in two enjoyable books. *Catalan Cuisine* (1988) by Colman Andrews is a lively mix of recipes, anecdotes and social comment, with notes on everything from *pa amb tomàquet* to the annual pig slaughter and how to make the perfect *allioli* sauce. *Barça: A People's Passion* (1999) by Jimmy Burns is a perceptive account of the first hundred years of FC Barcelona and its place in the Catalan nation.

The classic book on Barcelona is George Orwell's *Homage to Catalonia* (1938), which covers the Spanish Civil War from the perspective of a foreigner who volunteered for the republican militias. There are some good descriptions of Barcelona, but much of the book is taken up with a detailed account of the internecine struggles on the republican side, with communists fighting anarchists and Franco's nationalists reaping the rewards.

Finally, there is no better writer on modern Spain than Adam Hopkins, whose *Spanish Journeys* (1992) is a *tour de force* of Spanish history, art and architecture, including a detailed analysis of Barcelona's Modernist period.

Safety and security

Like any big city, Barcelona has its share of crime, though this mostly takes the form of petty annoyances rather than serious danger. The biggest problems are bag-snatching and pickpockets, so it pays to take a few common-sense precautions. Leave your passport, money and valuables in the hotel safe, and never carry around more cash than you need. In crowded places, keep your handbag firmly closed and avoid having a wallet in your back pocket. If you put down your bag or coat, leave it where you can see it, preferably on your lap, rather than slung over a chair in the street. There is no need to be paranoid, but it pays to be alert and aware of your surroundings and possessions at all times.

187

The lower end of La Rambla and the areas extending to either side, especially around Carrer dels Escudellers and the southern half of El Raval, have a **dangerous reputation**. There is no need to avoid these places, but it is wise to take extra care and to avoid dark alleyways late at night. Most of the characters who lurk here are seedy rather than dangerous, but wherever drugs and prostitution exist there is always an atmosphere of suppressed tension which makes some people feel uncomfortable.

If you are unlucky enough to be the victim of a crime, you will need to report it, if only for insurance purposes. Your first point of contact will usually be the **Policía Nacional**, who are responsible for dealing with serious crimes. They can be recognised on the street by their dark blue combat-style fatigues. A second police force, the **Policía Municipal** or **Guàrdia Urbana**, wear navy jackets and pale blue shirts and are responsible for traffic and enforcing law and order. In an emergency, you can contact the Policía Nacional on **091** or the Guàrdia Urbana on **092**. There is also a special tourist police service, **Turisme-Atenció** (*Rambla 43; tel: 93 301 9060*),

open 24 hours a day with multilingual officers to help tourists who need to report a crime.

Telephones

There are public telephones on virtually every street corner, with instructions in several languages. Most will accept coins, telephone cards and major credit cards. For international calls, the easiest option is to buy a **phonecard** (*tarjeta telefónica*), available in units of 1 000 or 2 000 ptas from post offices, news-stands and tobacconists'. These same outlets also sell a growing range of **pre-paid calling cards**, where you dial a toll-free number and enter a PIN (personal identification number) before making your call, which often works out cheaper. The cheap rate for international calls is from 2200 to 0800 on weekdays, after 1400 on Saturday and all day Sunday. Calls made from your hotel room are normally subject to a heavy surcharge.

All telephone numbers in Barcelona begin with the same area code, 93, followed by a seven-digit number. Before 1998, the area code could be omitted for local calls, but it now has to be dialled wherever you are calling from – so if you see a number with only seven digits, you probably need to add 93. For international calls, dial 00 followed by the code of the country you are calling (UK = 44, Ireland = 353, USA/Canada = 1) and then the area code, omitting the first zero in calls to the UK. To call Barcelona from abroad, dial the international access code (00 from the UK, 011 from the USA) followed by 34 for Spain and then the number listed in this book. A series of long tones means that the phone is ringing; short, rapid tones mean it is engaged. The usual greeting is *digame* ('speak to me').

Time

Spain is one hour ahead of GMT (Greenwich mean time) in winter and two hours ahead in summer, from the last Sunday in March to the last Sunday in October. The harmonisation of summer time across the European Union means that Spain is always one hour ahead of the UK.

Tipping

Most restaurant bills include a service charge, but it is usual to leave a small extra tip of around 5 per cent for good service. In bars, you usually pay for all drinks when you leave and it is customary to leave some small change on the counter. Taxi drivers expect around 10 per cent, and hotel porters, chambermaids and toilet attendants are always happy to receive a modest tip.

Toilets

A shortage of public toilets means that the easiest solution is usually to go into the nearest bar, where the price of a cup of coffee will save any potential embarrassment. Other good standbys are museums and department stores. If you need to ask for the toilet, the word is *la toaleta* in Catalan or *los servicios* in Spanish. The ideograms on the doors are usually self-explanatory, but if you are in any doubt the words are *caballeros* or *homes* for men and *señoras* or *dones* for women.

Travellers with disabilities

After a slow start, facilities for disabled people are improving rapidly in Spain, and all new public buildings have to be equipped with wheelchair access. Unfortunately, many of Barcelona's top sights, such as the Picasso Museum, are housed in older buildings that have not yet been fully adapted. The best advice is to ring before your visit so that your needs can be accommodated as far as possible.

Public transport is not yet fully accessible, though more and more Metro stations are introducing lifts and ramps, and adapted buses run on some routes. For the latest information, call the city information line (*tel: 010*) or pick up a transport map from the TMB office in Universitat Metro station, which lists wheelchair access points and wheelchair-friendly bus routes. Both the Aerobús and the Bus Turístic are accessible for disabled travellers. Taxis are legally obliged to carry wheelchairs and guide dogs, but some drivers are more willing than others. To book a minibus taxi equipped for wheelchair passengers, call Taxi Radio Móvil (*tel: 93 358 1111*) or Barnataxi (*tel: 93 357 7755*).

189

Index

Editorial, design and production credits

Project management: Dial House Publishing

Series editor: Christopher Catling

Proof-reader: Gill Colver

Series and cover design: Trickett & Webb Limited

Cover artwork: Wenham Arts

Text layout: Wenham Arts

Map work: Polly Senior Cartography

Repro and image setting: Z2 Repro, Thetford, Norfolk, UK

Printed and bound by: Artes Graficas ELKAR S. Coop., Bilbao, Spain

Acknowledgements

We would like to thank Neil Setchfield for the photographs used in this book, to whom the copyright belongs with the exception of the following:

J Allan Cash (page 146)

Greg Evans (page 162)

Robert Harding Picture Library (pages 42, 72, 108 and 130)

Paul Murphy (pages 6, 7, 9B, 10, 16A, 17A, 19, 33, 56, 62, 63A and B, 86, 105, 106, 107, 112, 114, 132, 136, 140, 141, 144, 145, 164, 168, 171B, 174A, 175, 183, 186 and 188A and B)

Spectrum (pages 154, 156, 157 and 161)

Telegraph Colour Library (page 47)